# PERSEVERANCE

## STAYING THE COURSE

## AT A GLANCE

**Serendipity House / P.O. Box 1012 / Littleton, CO 80160**
TOLL FREE 1-800-525-9563 / www.serendipityhouse.com
© 1989, 1998 Serendipity House. All rights reserved.
SECOND EDITION
00  01  02  03  04  / 201 series • CHG / 11  10  9  8  7  6  5

**PROJECT ENGINEER:**
Lyman Coleman

**WRITING TEAM:**
Richard Peace, Lyman Coleman, Matthew Lockhart, Andrew Sloan, Cathy Tardif

**PRODUCTION TEAM:**
Christopher Werner, Sharon Penington, Erika Tiepel

**COVER PHOTO:**
© 1998 W. Cody / Westlight

## CORE VALUES

**Community:** The purpose of this curriculum is to build community within the body of believers around Jesus Christ.

**Group Process:** To build community, the curriculum must be designed to take a group through a step-by-step process of sharing your story with one another.

**Interactive Bible Study:** To share your "story," the approach to Scripture in the curriculum needs to be open-ended and right brain—to "level the playing field" and encourage everyone to share.

**Developmental Stages:** To provide a healthy program in the life cycle of a group, the curriculum needs to offer courses on three levels of commitment: (1) Beginner Stage—low-level entry, high structure, to level the playing field; (2) Growth Stage—deeper Bible study, flexible structure, to encourage group accountability; (3) Discipleship Stage—in-depth Bible study, open structure, to move the group into high gear.

**Target Audiences:** To build community throughout the culture of the church, the curriculum needs to be flexible, adaptable and transferable into the structure of the average church.

## ACKNOWLEDGMENTS

To Zondervan Bible Publishers
for permission to use
the NIV text,
*The Holy Bible, New International Bible Society.*
© 1973, 1978, 1984 by International Bible Society.
Used by permission of Zondervan Bible Publishers.

# Questions & Answers

**STAGE**

1. *What stage in the life cycle of a small group is this course designed for?*

   Turn to the first page of the center section of this book. There you will see that this 201 course is designed for the second stage of a small group. In the Serendipity "Game Plan" for the multiplication of small groups, your group is in the Growth Stage.

**GOALS**

2. *What are the goals of a 201 study course?*

   As shown on the second page of the center section (page M2), the focus in this second stage is equally balanced between Spiritual Formation, Group Building, and Mission / Multiplication.

**BIBLE STUDY**

3. *What is the approach to Bible Study in this course?*

   Take a look at page M3 of the center section. The objective in a 201 course is to discover what a book of the Bible, or a series of related Scripture passages, has to say to our lives today. We will study each passage seriously, but with a strong emphasis on practical application to daily living.

**FOUR-STAGE LIFE CYCLE OF A GROUP**

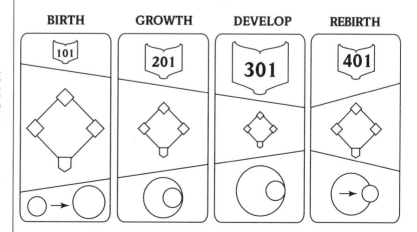

**GROUP BUILDING**

**4. *What is the meaning of the baseball diamond on pages M2 and M3 in relation to Group Building?***

Every Serendipity course includes group building. First base is where we share our own stories; second base means affirming one another's stories; third base is sharing our personal needs; and home plate is deeply caring for each others' needs. In this 201 course we will continue "checking in" with each other and holding each other accountable to live the Christian life.

**MISSION / MULTIPLICATION**

**5. *What is the mission of a 201 group?***

The mission of this 201 Covenant group is to discover the future leaders for starting a new group. (See graph on the previous page.) During this course, you will be challenged to identify three people and let this team use the Bible Study time to practice their skills. The center section will give you more details.

**THE EMPTY CHAIR**

**6. *How do we fill "the empty chair"?***

First, pull up an empty chair during the group's prayer time and ask God to bring a new person to the group to fill it. Second, have everyone make a prospect list of people they could invite and keep this list on their refrigerator until they have contacted all those on their list.

**AGENDA**

**7. *What is the agenda for our group meetings?***

A three-part agenda is found at the beginning of each session. Following the agenda and the recommended amount of time will keep your group on track and will keep the three goals of Spiritual Formation, Group Building, and Mission / Multiplication in balance.

## SUBGROUPING

If you have nine or more people at a meeting, Serendipity recommends you divide into groups of 4–6 for the Bible Study. Count off around the group: "one, two, one, two, etc."—and have the "ones" move quickly to another room for the Bible Study. Ask one person to be the leader and follow the directions for the Bible Study time. After 30 minutes, the Group Leader will call "Time" and ask all subgroups to come together for the Caring Time.

**ICE-BREAKERS**

8. *How do we decide what ice-breakers to use to begin the meetings?*

   Page M7 of the center section contains an index of ice-breakers in four categories: (1) those for getting acquainted in the first session or when a new person comes to a meeting; (2) those for the middle sessions to help you report in to your group; (3) those for the latter sessions to affirm each other and assign roles in preparation for starting a new group in the future; and (4) those for evaluating and reflecting in the final session.

**GROUP COVENANT**

9. *What is a group covenant?*

   A group covenant is a "contract" that spells out your expectations and the ground rules for your group. It's very important that your group discuss these issues—preferably as part of the first session (see also page M32 in the center section).

**GROUND RULES**

10. *What are the ground rules for the group?* (Check those you agree upon.)

    ❒ PRIORITY: While you are in the course, you give the group meetings priority.

    ❒ PARTICIPATION: Everyone participates and no one dominates.

    ❒ RESPECT: Everyone is given the right to their own opinion and all questions are encouraged and respected.

    ❒ CONFIDENTIALITY: Anything that is said in the meeting is never repeated outside the meeting.

    ❒ EMPTY CHAIR: The group stays open to new people at every meeting.

    ❒ SUPPORT: Permission is given to call upon each other in time of need—even in the middle of the night.

    ❒ ADVICE GIVING: Unsolicited advice is not allowed.

    ❒ MISSION: We agree to do everything in our power to start a new group as our mission (see center section).

# Introduction to 1 Peter

## The General Epistles

First Peter is one of the General Epistles. In addition to 1 Peter, six other books are included in this category: 2 Peter, Jude, James, and 1, 2 and 3 John. They were given this designation because it was felt that these letters were universal in scope. They were written to all churches and not just to a particular church (or person), as were Paul's letters.

However, this is not a completely accurate designation. Both James and 1 Peter are written to specific (though widely scattered) groups of Christians, and 2 and 3 John are addressed to very particular audiences (a specific church in one case and a specific person in the other).

## Audience

First Peter is a circular letter written to Christians living in the northwest section of Asia Minor (in what is now modern Turkey). In 1:1, Peter mentions Pontus, Galatia, Cappadocia, Asia and Bithynia (all of which are Roman provinces). This was a huge area with a large population. The fact that there were Christians living throughout the region testifies to the success of the early Christian missionaries.

The Christians to whom Peter writes were mainly Gentiles, as is clear from the way in which he describes their preconversion lifestyle. Peter uses categories and phrases that typically were applied to pagans, not Jews (see 1:14; 2:9–10; 4:3–4). Peter also uses the Greek form of his name in this letter, and not "Simeon," his Jewish name (as in Acts 15:14).

## Occasion

Peter wrote this letter to bring hope and strength to men and women who were being persecuted because they were Christians. At the time he wrote, such harassment was new. For the first three decades of its existence, the church was protected, not persecuted, by the Roman Empire. Christianity was seen as a Jewish sect and Judaism was recognized as a legitimate religion.

All this changed on July 19, A. D. 64. That night, Rome caught fire. For three days and three nights the fire blazed out of control. Ancient temples and historic landmarks were swept away by the ferocity of the blaze. Homes were destroyed. Ten of the 14 wards in the city suffered damage; three were reduced to rubble. The citizens of Rome were distraught and they were angry. They were angry because it was widely felt that Nero, the emperor, was the one responsible for the fire. If he had not actually started it (and there was evidence he did), he certainly had done nothing to contain it. In fact, Suetonius, the Roman historian, wrote that Nero "set fire to the city so openly that several former consuls did not venture to lay hands on his chamberlains although they caught them on their estates with tow and firebands."

Why would Nero burn down the city? Many felt that his passion for building led him to destroy Rome so that he could rebuild it. Nero tried to squelch the rumors about his part in the fire. He provided generous aid to the homeless and he did rebuild the city, this time with parks, wide streets, and buildings constructed of fireproof material. Still the rumors persisted. In desperation, Nero created a scapegoat. He blamed the fire on the Christians. In so doing, Nero introduced the church to martyrdom. The persecution that began in Rome would soon spread across the empire.

Why were Christians chosen to be the scapegoats? One reason probably had to do with anti-Semitism. The Jews were not popular in first-century Rome, and Christianity was considered to be a Jewish sect. Another reason had to do with rumors that were circulating about Christian rites. Some said that Christians were cannibals (who each week ate somebody's body and drank someone's blood). Others accused them of orgies, misunderstanding what the Agape (or Love) Feast was all about.

In any case, the persecution directed at Christians was savage. Tacitus, another Roman historian, wrote about the events in that day:

Neither human resources, nor imperial munificence, nor appeasement of the gods, eliminated sinister suspicions that the fire had been instigated. To suppress this rumor, Nero fabricated scapegoats—and punished with every refinement the notoriously depraved Christians (as they were popularly called) ... First, Nero had self-acknowledged Christians arrested. Then, on their information, large numbers of others were condemned—not so much for incendiarism as for their anti-social tendencies. Their deaths were made farcical. Dressed in wild animals' skins, they were torn to pieces by dogs, or crucified, or made into torches to be ignited after dark as substitutes for daylight. Nero provided his Gardens for the spectacle ... Despite their guilt as Christians, and the ruthless punishment it deserved, the victims were pitied. For it was felt that they were being sacrificed to one man's brutality rather than to the national interest.

Under Roman law, there were two types of religious systems: those that were legal (such as Judaism) and those that were forbidden. Anyone who practiced a forbidden religion was considered a criminal and was subject to harsh penalties. After the Great Fire, Christianity was declared to be a forbidden religion. This meant that, throughout the empire, Christians were now technically outlaws and thus subject to persecution. Peter writes to those Christians in Asia Minor who were going through such persecution.

## Purpose

Peter wrote this letter to comfort and encourage these Asian Christians in the midst of the "painful trial" (4:12) they were undergoing. He says to them: "Rejoice that you participate in the sufferings of Christ" (4:13). At first glance, this seems to be a strange thing to say. How can they rejoice when times are so tough? The answer Peter gives is that rejoicing is possible because of the great hope they have as Christians. Hope is the theme of Peter's letter to these suffering Christians.

## Style

First Peter is written in excellent Greek, so much so that some have questioned whether a Galilean fisherman like Peter could have had such a sophisticated command of the language. First Peter contains some of the best Greek in the New Testament—"smoother and more literary than that of the highly trained Paul" (Beare)—with a rhythmic structure not unlike that found in the writings of the Greek masters.

As it turns out, this good Greek probably came from a man by the name of Silas (or Silvanus). As Peter says in 5:12: "With the help of Silas ... I have written to you." The way the Greek is phrased in 5:12 indicates that Silas was more than a mere stenographer. He could well be the one who helped Peter to polish up the language and style as he dictated the letter. "The thought is the thought of Peter; but the style is the style of Silvanus" (Barclay).

## Sources

When reading 1 Peter, one keeps hearing echoes from other parts of the Bible. Certainly the Old Testament is one source which Peter drew upon. He quotes a number of passages, particularly from Isaiah (e.g., 1:24–25a; 2:6,8,22 where he quotes Isa. 40:6–8; 28:16; 8:14; 53:9). Furthermore, he makes a lot of allusions to Old Testament ideas and stories (e.g., in 1:19 and 2:4–10, which parallel Isa. 53).

Peter also seems to be familiar with the writings of Paul. There are parallels to Romans and, in particular, to Ephesians (e.g. compare 1 Peter 1:3 with Eph. 1:3 and compare 1 Peter 1:20 with Eph. 1:4; furthermore, the instructions to slaves, husbands, and wives are similar to what is found in Eph. 5–6). In addition, there are parallels to Hebrews and James. Not surprisingly, the clearest parallels are to Peter's sermons in Acts. Selwyn has shown that the theology of 1 Peter parallels exactly the theology in these sermons.

Of course, this does not necessarily mean that Peter was consciously quoting from New Testament documents. What he is echoing may simply be the common pattern of teaching in the early church into which he is tapping, as did other New Testament writers.

## Date

As with most other ancient letters, it is not possible to give a precise date for the composition of 1 Peter. However, if this letter was sparked by Nero's persecution (and if Peter died in Rome in A.D. 68 as tradition has it), then it must have been written in the mid-60s.

## Outline

I.  Greetings (1:1–2)

II.  The Identity and Hope of the People of God (1:3–2:10)

   A. A Great Salvation (1:3–12)

   B. A New Lifestyle (1:13–25)

   C. A Chosen Priesthood (2:1–10)

III.  The Responsibilities of the People of God (2:11–4:11)

   A. The Mission of God's People (2:11–12)

   B. Respect: The Key to a Missionary Lifestyle (2:13–3:12)

   C. The Promise of Vindication (3:13–4:6)

   D. Love: The Key to an Eschatological Lifestyle (4:7–11)

IV.  The Present Challenge to the People of God (4:12–5:14)

   A. The Fiery Trial (4:12–19)

   B. The Responsibilities of a Church Under Judgment (5:1–11)

   C. Conclusion (5:12–14)

# 1 Salutation—1 Peter 1:1-2

## THREE-PART AGENDA

**ICE-BREAKER**
15 Minutes

**BIBLE STUDY**
30 Minutes

**CARING TIME**
15–45 Minutes

> *LEADER: Be sure to read pages 3–5 in the front of this book, and go over the ground rules on page 5 with the group in this first session. See page M7 in the center section for a good ice-breaker. Have your group look at pages M1–M5 in the center section and fill out the team roster on page M5.*

## TO BEGIN THE BIBLE STUDY TIME
(Choose 1 or 2)

1. How many times did your family move when you were growing up? Which time was the hardest?

2. How geographically scattered is your extended family now? How often do you get together?

3. Who is the person that you correspond with most often?

## READ SCRIPTURE & DISCUSS
(If you don't have time for all the questions in this section, conclude the Bible Study [30 min.] by answering question #7.)

1. When have you most felt like a stranger: As a result of relocating? Changing schools? Changing jobs? Other?

2. What do you remember about the apostle Peter, the writer of this letter? (For more information on Peter, see note on verse 1.)

3. In what sense are "God's elect, strangers in the world" (v. 1)? When have you most felt like a stranger because of your faith? What gets you through those times?

**1** *Peter, an apostle of Jesus Christ,*

*To God's elect, strangers in the world, scattered through-out Pontus, Galatia, Cappadocia, Asia and Bithynia, ²who have been chosen according to the foreknowledge of God the Father, through the sanctifying work of the Spirit, for obedience to Jesus Christ and sprinkling by his blood:*

*Grace and peace be yours in abundance.*

4. For what purpose have God's elect been chosen?

5. What does it mean to you to be chosen by God? To be sanctified by the Spirit? To be sprinkled by Christ's blood?

6. As you begin this course, how full does your "grace meter" read: Full? Half-full? Empty? Overflowing? Other?

7. What brought you to this study and what are you hoping to get out of it?

## CARING TIME

1. Have your group agree on its group covenant and ground rules (see page 5 in the front of this book).

2. Work on filling out your team roster (see page M5 in the center section). Like any winning team, every position needs to be covered.

3. Who is someone you would like to invite to this group for next week?

*P.S. At the close, pass around your books and have everyone sign the Group Directory inside the front cover.*

Share prayer requests and close in prayer. Be sure to pray for "the empty chair" (p. 4).

**1:1–2** Peter begins his letter in the way most Greek letters began in the first century. He first identifies himself as the writer and then identifies those to whom his letter is written. He concludes the salutation with his own version of the standard Christian greeting: "Grace and peace be yours in abundance."

In the process of identifying those to whom he is writing, Peter gives us rich insight into what it means to be a Christian. In relationship to God, Christians are "elect." They are chosen by the Father; this choice is activated by the Holy Spirit and it is made possible by the Son. (This is an early formulation of the doctrine of the Trinity.) In relationship to the world, Christians are "strangers," "scattered" throughout the world.

**1:1 *Peter.*** Peter was the leader of the 12 apostles. Before joining Jesus' band of disciples he was a fisherman on the Sea of Galilee. He worked with his brother Andrew in partnership with James and John (Luke 5:10). Their business was based in Capernaum where Peter and Andrew lived together (Mark 1:21,29). Peter was married (Mark 1:30). Later in his ministry he took his wife with him on visits to the churches (1 Cor. 9:5). His father's name was Jonah (Matt. 16:17). Peter, along with his brother Andrew, was one of the first chosen to be a disciple of Jesus (Mark 1:16–18).

Peter was the most prominent of the disciples. In every list of the Twelve, he is mentioned first. The reason for this is clear. Peter often took the initiative in situations (as when he volunteered to walk to Jesus across the water—Matt. 14:28). He generally spoke for the disciples (as at Caesarea Philippi when he answered Jesus' question about who he was—Mark 8:29). Peter was also part of the inner circle of disciples (Peter, James and John) with whom Jesus had the most intimate relationship. He was the first of the Twelve to see the resurrected Jesus (1 Cor. 15:5). During the early years after the Resurrection, Peter was the dominant force in the church. He was a powerful preacher through whom thousands came to faith (Acts 2:14–41); he worked miracles, including raising a woman from the dead (Acts 9:36–42); he spearheaded outreach to Jews living outside Jerusalem (Acts 8:14; 9:32–35); and he was responsible for allowing Gentiles to be baptized without first converting to Judaism (Acts 10:1–11:18). The first 12 chapters of Acts focus on his role in the early church. Tradition has it that Peter was crucified upside-down in Rome in the mid to late A.D. 60s.

Peter is known by four names in the New Testament: Simeon, his Hebrew name (Acts 15:14); Simon, a Greek name (e.g., Mark 1:16); Peter, the name that Jesus gave to him (John 1:42) and which he uses here; and Cephas which is the Aramaic version of Peter. Peter is his "Christian" name and means "a stone" or "a rock."

> *The choice of God takes effect by the work of the Holy Spirit. The aim of the work of the Spirit is holiness. The Holy Spirit awakens in people the longing for God.*

***an apostle.*** This means, literally, "one who is sent." It is the term used in the New Testament to identify those who were selected for the special task of founding and guiding the new church. To be an apostle one had to be a witness to the resurrection of Jesus.

***To God's elect.*** To be "elect" is to be chosen by God to be a member of his family. Deuteronomy 7:6 expresses this: "The Lord your God has chosen you out of all the peoples on the face of the earth to be his people, his treasured possession." "The elect" had once been a phrase reserved for the nation of Israel, but after Jesus' death and resurrection it was used to refer to the church.

***strangers in the world.*** The Greek word used here is *parepidemoi.* It means "sojourner" and refers to those who are far from home, dwelling in a strange land. The term is used metaphorically for Christians, whose true home is in heaven.

***scattered.*** The Greek word here is *diaspora,* which means "the dispersion." It originally referred to those Jews who were scattered in exile throughout a number of countries outside Palestine. Once again, Peter uses a term originally applied to Israel to refer to the church.

**Pontus, Galatia, Cappadocia, Asia and Bithynia.** These are Roman provinces located in Asia Minor (now modern Turkey). The order in which they are named is the order in which a traveler would visit each.

**1:2** Peter has already referred to the Christians as "God's elect." In this verse he points out the role of God the Father, God the Son, and God the Holy Spirit in the process of election. The doctrine of the Trinity emerged out of the experience of the people.

**chosen according to the foreknowledge of God the Father.** Israel knew itself to be chosen (selected, elected, picked) by God to be his people (Ezek. 20:5; Hos. 11:1). They were to be the people through whom he would reveal himself to the rest of the world. The first Christians knew that they too had been chosen by God (see notes on 2:4 and 2:9–10).

**foreknowledge.** It is not just a matter of God knowing something before it happens. What God foreknows he brings to pass. Here his purpose is defined as "obedience to Jesus."

**the sanctifying work of the Spirit.** The choice of God takes effect by the work of the Holy Spirit. The aim of the work of the Spirit is holiness. The Holy Spirit awakens in people the longing for God, convicts them of their sin, and opens them to the saving power of Jesus' death. Following conversion, the Spirit continues this sanctifying work by bringing power to overcome sin, assurance of sins forgiven, and new ways of living and feeling (the fruit of the Spirit).

**sanctifying.** To sanctify is to make holy. (The word "holiness" and the word "sanctification" both come from the same Greek root.) To be holy is not to be some sort of especially pious person (this is the common misunderstanding of the word). It is to be set apart for God and thus to reflect his nature.

**for obedience to Jesus Christ.** The aim of this chosenness is obedience to Christ. The obedience referred to here is not the daily obedience of the believer. "It denotes his once-for-all obedience which led to his acceptance of reconciliation through the blood of Jesus Christ" (Best).

**sprinkling by his blood.** It is by means of the death of Christ that election is made possible. His death opened the way back to God. The image of sprinkling with blood comes from the Jewish sacrificial system. The primary Old Testament reference is to the acceptance of the covenant by the people of Israel (see Ex. 24:1–8). God expressed his choice of Israel by means of a covenant in which he agreed to be their God and they agreed to obey him. Moses took half the blood of the sacrificial animals and sprinkled it on the altar and the other half on the people, thus sealing their commitment.

**Grace and peace.** At this point in a letter, the typical Greek writer would usually say simply: "Greetings." However, Peter and other New Testament writers (e.g Paul, see Phil. 1:2) Christianized this statement. First, they transformed the Greek for "greetings" to "grace," a related word from the same Greek root. Then they added the Hebrew greeting "shalom," which in Greek became "peace." There are some differences, however, between this greeting by Peter and what Paul usually says. Paul generally points out that this grace and peace comes from God.

# 2 A Living Hope—1 Peter 1:3–12

## THREE-PART AGENDA

| ICE-BREAKER | BIBLE STUDY | CARING TIME |
|---|---|---|
| 15 Minutes | 30 Minutes | 15–45 Minutes |

>  **LEADER: If there's a new person in your group in this session, start with an ice-breaker (see page M7 in the center section).** Then begin the session with a word of prayer. If you have more than nine in your group, see the box about the "Subgrouping" on page 4. Count off around the group: "one, two, one, two, etc."—and have the "ones" move quickly to another room for the Bible Study.

## TO BEGIN THE BIBLE STUDY TIME
(Choose 1 or 2)

1. Who in this group has had the most broken bones?

2. What do you like to do to celebrate really good news?

3. What is something for which you are particularly thankful?

## READ SCRIPTURE & DISCUSS
(If you don't have time for all the questions in this section, conclude the Bible Study [30 min.] by answering question #7.)

1. When you were growing up, what was the worst trial your family ever faced?

2. What does Peter mean by the "new birth" that God provides (see second note on v. 3)? How did your life change when you encountered Christ?

3. What purpose do trials serve in a Christian's life? In what can you "greatly rejoice" (v. 6) despite the trials you face?

Praise to God for a Living Hope

*³Praise be to the God and Father of our Lord Jesus Christ! In his great mercy he has given us new birth into a living hope through the resurrection of Jesus Christ from the dead, ⁴and into an inheritance that can never perish, spoil or fade—kept in heaven for you, ⁵who through faith are shielded by God's power until the coming of the salvation that is ready to be revealed in the last time. ⁶In this you greatly rejoice, though now for a little while you may have had to suffer grief in all kinds of trials. ⁷These have come so that your faith—of greater worth than gold, which perishes even though refined by fire—may be proved genuine and may result in praise, glory and honor when Jesus Christ is revealed. ⁸Though you have not seen him, you love him; and even though you do not see him now, you believe in him and are filled with an inexpressible and glorious joy, ⁹for you are receiving the goal of your faith, the salvation of your souls.*

*¹⁰Concerning this salvation, the prophets, who spoke of the grace that was to come to you, searched intently and with the greatest care, ¹¹trying to find out the time and circumstances to which the Spirit of Christ in them was pointing when he predicted the sufferings of Christ and the glories that would follow. ¹²It was revealed to them that they were not serving themselves but you, when they spoke of the things that have now been told you by those who have preached the gospel to you by the Holy Spirit sent from heaven. Even angels long to look into these things.*

4. What perspective does Peter give suffering in verses 6–7? How does this perspective help you deal with past or current suffering in your life?

5. Even though those Peter was writing to were suffering persecution, how does he describe their spiritual relationship and outlook (vv. 8–9)? What does your outlook tend to be when you're "under fire"?

6. When has your faith been tested by a fiery trial? How did you come out of it? What are you going through right now that is helping to strengthen your faith?

7. Which point from this passage do you need the most right now: A new birth? Hope for the future? Faith in God's power? Joy regardless of circumstances? Love for the "unseen" Jesus?

*P.S. Add new group members to the Group Directory inside the front cover.*

## CARING TIME
(Choose 1 or 2 of these questions before closing in prayer. Be sure to pray for the empty chair.)

1. How are you doing at inviting others to the group? Who could you invite for next week?

2. How do you feel about sharing your struggles with this group?

3. How can the group pray for you this week?

**Summary.** Typically in a Greek letter, the salutation is followed by a word of thanksgiving to the gods for blessings received. Peter follows this pattern and in these verses praises God for the resurrection of Jesus Christ through which salvation came (vv. 3–5). The reality of this salvation brings rejoicing, which in turn upholds the church in the trials it must face until Jesus returns (vv. 6–9). He ends his prayer by recalling the long preparation for this salvation in the history of Israel (vv. 10–12).

Thus Peter picks up on the themes found in his salutation and here spells out in more detail the identity of the people of God. The basis for their identity is the great salvation that God is bringing about. This salvation will be consummated in the future (vv. 3–5), though it is present in their daily experience (vv. 6–9) and it is rooted in the past (vv. 10–12).

**1:3–5** Peter begins his letter with a powerful statement in which he focuses on the coming day of salvation. As Barclay says: "There are few passages in the New Testament where more of the great fundamental Christian ideas and conceptions meet and come together." Two facts are singled out here for note. God has *redeemed* them and he has *guarded* them so that they will receive the full benefit of their salvation.

**1:3** *Praise be.* The phrase "praise be" or "blessed be" followed by the name of God was common in Jewish prayers (see Ps. 68:19). It later was adopted by the Christian church (see 2 Cor. 1:3) and is used here by Peter.

*new birth.* When people encounter Jesus, something so radical happens that they can be said to be reborn into a whole new life. This is no mere metaphor, but an accurate description of the transformation whereby a person becomes a part of the family of God and aware of spiritual reality.

*a living hope.* This is the first thing new birth brings. Specifically here, their hope is that one day when Christ comes again they will experience the full fruit of salvation when they experience the resurrection life of Jesus. They have tasted this new life in the here and now, but they have not yet come into full possession of it. It is this hope that sustains them in hard times.

*the resurrection of Jesus.* That which makes salvation possible is the fact that Jesus rose from the dead and lives today as the powerful Lord of heaven and earth. His resurrection from death to life makes possible their rebirth to spiritual life. "Christ's resurrection is the ground and guarantee of our resurrection hope" (Kelly).

**1:4** *into an inheritance.* New birth also brings a secure inheritance. To be born again means they have become part of a new family, and like all sons and daughters they can expect an inheritance.

*never perish, spoil or fade.* The first phrase, "never perish," can also mean "unravaged by any invading army" (Barclay). The second phrase, "never spoil," refers to a land that has not been polluted or defiled by a conquering army. The third phrase, "never fade," paints a picture of a land without change or decay. It refers especially to flowers that do not fade. Taken together, these descriptions define a land that is radically different from the Promised Land that time and again was conquered, despoiled and desecrated. In contrast, heaven ... "is untouched by death, unstained by evil, unimpaired by time" (Beare).

*kept in heaven for you.* This inheritance is immune to disaster.

**1:5** *shielded.* Not only is the inheritance guarded and immune to disaster, but so too are the Christians for whom it exists.

> *That which makes salvation possible is the fact that Jesus rose from the dead and lives today as the powerful Lord of heaven and earth. His resurrection from death to life makes possible their rebirth to spiritual life. "Christ's resurrection is the ground and guarantee of our resurrection hope."*

**salvation.** This is the object of the believers' hope and the content of their inheritance. The word "salvation" is used in several ways in the New Testament. The reference here is not to individual salvation, but to that moment in history when Christ will return again and all believers will come into the full enjoyment of eternity.

**1:6** The experience of rebirth and the anticipation of an inheritance (both fruits of salvation) enable Christians to "greatly rejoice" despite trials and adversities. They know that these trials are only temporary (as stated here in v. 6), that they will get through them (v. 5), and that what lies ahead is the most real of all (v. 4). They can stand anything now because of what is theirs in the future.

*for a little while you may have had to suffer.* By these two clauses, Peter gives perspective to their suffering. First, it will be temporary ("for a little while"). He may say this because he feels that the Lord's coming is near, or because in comparison with eternity what they are going through is but a moment. Second, such trials are circumstantial, perhaps even necessary ("you may have had to" or "if need be"). Trials simply come. Certain circumstances make them inevitable. However, such trials do not fall outside God's providence.

*grief.* This stands in contrast to "rejoice." Within the trials there is both real grief and authentic rejoicing.

*trials.* Peter's first allusion to their persecution. The language indicates that he has in mind actual difficulties they have faced and are facing.

**1:7** Peter adds a third perspective. They can endure because these trials will have a positive benefit. They will reveal the quality of their faith.

*gold.* Gold was the most precious of metals in the first century. Their faith is worth even more!

*fire.* Fire was used to burn away the impurities and so reveal the pure gold. In the same way, trials reveal the inner quality of faith. In an interesting twist, Peter notes that even though gold can stand up to fire, in the end it too, as part of the creation, will perish.

*proved genuine.* This will make evident the actual quality and strength of the faith they possess. Such trials do not create faith; they reveal what is already there.

**1:8** Most of the Christians to whom Peter writes would not have known Jesus when he was alive. But that doesn't matter. They still love him and have faith in him, with the result that they are filled with an overwhelming joy.

*glorious.* This joy is "shot through with the radiance which belongs to God's very essence and which he imparts to his chosen" (Kelly).

**1:9** *for you are receiving.* The verb means, literally, "carry off for oneself," and refers to a prize or a punishment one has earned. The tense of the verb indicates that this is a present reality. They are even now experiencing the salvation which they will fully realize only in the future.

**1:10–12** The salvation that is still to come (vv. 3–5) and which is present even now (vv. 6–9) was in the past the object of longing on the part of prophets (vv. 10–12a) and even angels (v. 12b).

**1:11** *trying to find.* In the era preceding Jesus, there was frantic seeking to know what God would do. Even the Old Testament prophets, as Peter points out here, had only a blurred vision of what was to come in God's grace.

*the Spirit of Christ.* The pre-existent Christ was the one who inspired the prophets.

**1:12** The Old Testament looked forward to the New. There is a continuity and a unity between both parts of the Bible. What the prophets predicted was preached by the apostles.

*It was revealed.* The process of revelation involves the searching and probing of prophets, coupled with and guided by the leading of the Spirit. In this way God reveals himself.

# 3 Be Holy—1 Peter 1:13–2:3

## THREE-PART AGENDA

| ICE-BREAKER | BIBLE STUDY | CARING TIME |
|---|---|---|
| 15 Minutes | 30 Minutes | 15–45 Minutes |

>  **LEADER: Remember to choose an appropriate ice-breaker if you have a new person at the meeting (see page M7 in the center section), and then begin with a prayer. If you have more than nine in your group, divide into subgroups of 4–6 for the Bible Study (see the box about the "Subgrouping" on page 4).**

## TO BEGIN THE BIBLE STUDY TIME
(Choose 1 or 2)

1. How did you get ready for exams in school: Study regularly? Cram all night? Get a good night's sleep?

2. On a scale of 1 (totally disobedient) to 10 (totally obedient), what kind of a child were you?

3. Who do you know who is a "perfectionist"?

## READ SCRIPTURE & DISCUSS
(If you don't have time for all the questions in this section, conclude the Bible Study [30 min.] by answering question #7.)

1. What do most people today think of when they hear the word "holy" or "holiness"?

2. What kind of holiness does Peter call us to (see note on v. 15)? How does Peter's call to holiness in this passage challenge you at home, work, church or in your neighborhood?

3. How much trouble do you have being drawn back to the "evil desires you had when you lived in ignorance" before you were a Christian (v. 14)? How can focusing on what Jesus has done for you (vv. 18–21) help?

Be Holy

*[13] Therefore, prepare your minds for action; be self-controlled; set your hope fully on the grace to be given you when Jesus Christ is revealed. [14] As obedient children, do not conform to the evil desires you had when you lived in ignorance. [15] But just as he who called you is holy, so be holy in all you do; [16] for it is written: "Be holy, because I am holy."* a

*[17] Since you call on a Father who judges each man's work impartially, live your lives as strangers here in reverent fear. [18] For you know that it was not with perishable things such as silver or gold that you were redeemed from the empty way of life handed down to you from your forefathers, [19] but with the precious blood of Christ, a lamb without blemish or defect. [20] He was chosen before the creation of the world, but was revealed in these last times for your sake. [21] Through him you believe in God, who raised him from the dead and glorified him, and so your faith and hope are in God.*

*[22] Now that you have purified yourselves by obeying the truth so that you have sincere love for your brothers, love one another deeply, from the heart.* b *[23] For you have been born again, not of perishable seed, but of imperishable, through the living and enduring word of God. [24] For,*

*"All men are like grass,*
*and all their glory is like the flowers of the field;*
*the grass withers and the flowers fall,*
*[25] but the word of the Lord stands forever."* c

*And this is the word that was preached to you.*

**2** *Therefore, rid yourselves of all malice and all deceit, hypocrisy, envy, and slander of every kind. [2] Like newborn babies, crave pure spiritual milk, so that by it you may grow up in your salvation, [3] now that you have tasted that the Lord is good.*

a16 Lev. 11:44,45; 19:2; 20:7    b22 Some early manuscripts *from a pure heart*    c25 Isaiah 40:6–8

4. What does it mean to "live your lives as strangers here in reverent fear" (v. 17)? How common is that attitude today?

5. What is a good test to see if a person has really had a change of heart (v. 22)? What makes loving others deeply and actively possible (vv. 23–25)? What grade would you give yourself on loving others lately?

6. What is the "pure spiritual milk" we are to crave (see notes on v. 2)? In what way do you still need this milk?

7. From this passage, what do you need to do to live a holier life?

## CARING TIME
(Choose 1 or 2 of these questions before closing in prayer. Be sure to pray for the empty chair.)

1. If you were to describe the last week of your life in terms of weather, what was it like: Sunny and warm? Cold? Scattered showers? Other? What is the forecast for the coming week?

2. Does the group have a person for every position on the team roster (review p. M5)?

3. How can the group help you in prayer this week?

19

**Summary.** In this passage, Peter continues his discussion of who his readers are as the people of God. Their identity is not only derived from the fact of their salvation (1:3–12), but from the lifestyle that results from their experience of God's grace (1:13–25). This lifestyle involves three things: holiness (1:13–16), reverence (1:17–21) and love (1:22–25). Peter describes this lifestyle by means of a series of exhortations (1:13–15,17,22–23) based on Scripture (1:16,24–25) and on their experience (1:18–21). Peter moves from the great salvation they can look forward to in the future (1:3–12) to the battle of living which they face in the here and now (1:13–2:3).

**1:13 *Therefore.*** The salvation they have received results in a distinctive lifestyle involving clarity of mind, self-control, and an active hope. Given the severity of their situation, they cannot afford to act without thought, in an extreme or undisciplined way, or on the basis of despair.

***prepare your minds for action.*** This is the first of a series of imperatives (commands) in this passage. This phrase means literally "gird up the loins of your mind." It paints a picture of a man gathering up his long robe and tucking it in his belt ("girding up") so that he can run without hindrance. In order to live as they ought, they too must prepare themselves; specifically they need a clarity of mind. They must think about how they live and not merely react. This is a time for cool heads and carefully thought-through actions.

**1:14 *do not conform to the evil desires.*** They are not to allow themselves to be shaped by the sensuality of their pre-Christian existence. They might be tempted to go along with the norms of others and so not stand out as different, thus escaping notice in the persecution.

***ignorance.*** Not only was their pre-Christian life dominated by physical desires of all sorts, they also lived in ignorance of God. Pagans in the first century believed in God, but thought him to be unknowable and disinterested in human beings.

**1:15 *holy.*** The holiness to which Peter calls them is not ritual in nature (as it had become in Judaism) nor magical in content (as it was in paganism). As Kelly describes it, "God Himself, not any system of abstract ideals, much less rules, is to be their stan-

dard, for as a result of His calling He has made them His own ... [Holiness] connotes the freedom from sin and absolute moral integrity which fellowship with God makes imperative."

**1:16 *it is written.*** Peter appeals to Scripture for his authority to urge such holiness on them.

**1:17** God is both their Father and their Judge. On both counts their attitude ought to be one of "reverent fear."

***strangers.*** Christians are to make decisions not in terms of their present circumstances, but in the light of God's kingdom where their true home is found.

***reverent fear.*** What Peter encourages here is not so much fear as it is awe.

**1:18 *For you know that.*** Peter is referring to what they knew from creeds, catechism and liturgy. What Peter describes in the next few verses is the church's teaching on the redeeming work of Jesus.

***redeemed.*** To redeem someone is to rescue that person from bondage. This is a technical term for the money paid to buy freedom for a slave.

**1:19** The price of their ransom from their pagan lifestyle was not material ("silver or gold") but spiritual (the "blood of Christ"). Here, Peter refers to Jesus in sacrificial terms as the innocent victim dying in place of others.

***blood.*** In the Old Testament, the blood of the sacrificial animal was offered to God in place of the life of the sinner. In the New Testament, it is not the sacrifice of animals that secures forgiveness; it is the death of Jesus who gave himself once for all.

***without blemish or defect.*** Jesus was able to be such a sacrifice because he was without sin. This is a remarkable confession from one like Peter who lived in close contact with Jesus for three years. Of all people, Peter would have been able to point out sin in Jesus' life, had there been any.

**1:21 *Through him you believe in God.*** Yet another aspect of Christ's work: they came to belief in the true and living God via Jesus. In Jesus they saw and understood who God was.

**raised him from the dead and glorified him.** Jesus' redemptive work began with the Cross, but was not complete until he was resurrected and glorified. Crucifixion, resurrection and glorification are all part of one event.

**faith and hope.** Their faith (trust) and hope is that they, too, will share in the resurrection life of Jesus and in the glory that is his.

**1:22 purified / obeying.** Purification comes from obedience, and this issues in love for others. In the Old Testament, there was a ritual purification of objects and people so as to fit them for the service of God (see Num. 8:21; 31:23). In the New Testament, purification is of a moral nature. Christians are called upon to rid themselves of those vices, passions and negative attitudes (see 2:1) that make it difficult to love others.

**sincere love.** The word Peter uses for love is *philadelphia* (not *agape*) and refers to love between Christian brothers and sisters.

**1:23–25** Peter contrasts human and divine birth (perishable seed vs. imperishable seed) in order to explain the origin of this new community.

**2:1** They are to rid themselves of all those behaviors which work against brotherly love. The list Peter uses here is similar to other such vice lists in the New Testament (e.g., Rom. 1:29–30; Eph. 4:31).

**rid yourselves.** This verb was used to describe taking off one's clothes. They must strip off, like spoiled and dirty clothes, their old lifestyle.

**all malice and all deceit.** These are general terms which refer to attitudes that disrupt a community.

**hypocrisy, envy, and slander.** Specific vices that make relationships difficult. Hypocrites pretend to be one thing while, in fact, they are concealing their true motives. Envy is jealousy of another's place and privilege. Slander involves speaking evil of others when they are not there to defend themselves.

**2:2** Having rid themselves of the old ways, they are like newborn babies. They need pure milk which will nourish them so that they grow to maturity.

> *Christians are to make decisions not in terms of their present circumstances, but in the light of God's kingdom where their true home is found.*

**crave.** Having described them as newborn babies, he continues the metaphor by drawing upon the idea of the strong, natural, instinctive desire that infants have for milk.

**pure.** This is the first of two adjectives that describe the milk they are to crave. In Greek the word is *adolos* and it means "free from deceit." It is set in contrast to the deceit (*dolos*) they are to rid themselves of (2:1).

**milk.** That the milk to which Peter refers is the Word of God is supported by two other references in the New Testament (1 Cor. 3:2; Heb. 5:12–14). In both cases, religious instruction is referred to as "milk," and emphasizes that the source of teaching for Christians is the Scripture.

**2:3** In the end, however, it is not words about Christ that sustain them; it is Christ himself. They have "tasted that the Lord is good" (Ps. 34:8).

## THREE-PART AGENDA

| ICE-BREAKER | BIBLE STUDY | CARING TIME |
|---|---|---|
| 15 Minutes | 30 Minutes | 15–45 Minutes |

*LEADER: If there's a new person in this session, start with an ice-breaker from the center section (see page M7). Remember to stick closely to the three-part agenda and the time allowed for each segment. Is your group praying for the empty chair? As the leader, you may want to choose question #2 in the Caring Time to facilitate the group in handling accountability issues.*

## TO BEGIN THE BIBLE STUDY TIME
(Choose 1 or 2)

1. What clubs, teams, groups or organizations are you a member of?

2. As a kid, how were sides chosen on the playground? When were you usually picked?

3. What's something you've made or built recently?

## READ SCRIPTURE & DISCUSS
(If you don't have time for all the questions in this section, conclude the Bible Study [30 min.] by answering question #7.)

1. If you were to design your "dream house," what one or two special features would it have?

2. What process is God undertaking in the lives of believers? What does it mean to you to be part of this "spiritual house" (v. 5)?

3. In what ways is Christ "A stone that causes men to stumble" (v. 8)?

### The Living Stone and a Chosen People

*⁴As you come to him, the living Stone—rejected by men but chosen by God and precious to him— ⁵you also, like living stones, are being built into a spiritual house to be a holy priesthood, offering spiritual sacrifices acceptable to God through Jesus Christ. ⁶For in Scripture it says:*

> *"See, I lay a stone in Zion,*
> > *a chosen and precious cornerstone,*
> *and the one who trusts in him*
> > *will never be put to shame."*ᵃ

*⁷Now to you who believe, this stone is precious. But to those who do not believe,*

> *"The stone the builders rejected*
> > *has become the capstone,*ᵇ*"*ᶜ

*⁸and,*

> *"A stone that causes men to stumble*
> > *and a rock that makes them fall."*ᵈ

*They stumble because they disobey the message—which is also what they were destined for.*

*⁹But you are a chosen people, a royal priesthood, a holy nation, a people belonging to God, that you may declare the praises of him who called you out of darkness into his wonderful light. ¹⁰Once you were not a people, but now you are the people of God; once you had not received mercy, but now you have received mercy.*

*¹¹Dear friends, I urge you, as aliens and strangers in the world, to abstain from sinful desires, which war against your soul. ¹²Live such good lives among the pagans that, though they accuse you of doing wrong, they may see your good deeds and glorify God on the day he visits us.*

ᵃ6 Isaiah 28:16   ᵇ7 Or *cornerstone*   ᶜ7 Psalm 118:22   ᵈ8 Isaiah 8:14

4. How does it make you feel to know you are chosen by God—that you belong to him (see vv. 9–10)?

5. By what various names does Peter call Christians in this passage? Which of these terms can you relate to the most?

6. According to verses 11–12, how is our new status with God to influence the way we live?

7. What has your "spiritual house" (v. 5) felt like lately: A secure castle? A leaky hut? A construction site? Other?

## CARING TIME

(Choose 1 or 2 of these questions before closing in prayer. Be sure to pray for the empty chair.)

1. How is your relationship with God right now: Close? Distant? Improving? Strained? Other?

2. For what would you like this group to help hold you accountable?

3. How can the group support you in prayer this week?

**Summary.** Thus far Peter has pointed out two things about the identity of the people of God: (1) who they are is grounded in their experience of salvation (1:3–12), and (2) who they are is expressed in the kind of life they lead (1:13–2:3). Here he adds a third point: they have a special task. He uses two metaphors to describe this role: (1) they are *living stones* who are being built up into a spiritual house (vv. 4–8), and (2) they are a *royal priesthood* who declare the praises of God (vv. 9–12). As in the previous passage, Peter begins and ends with exhortations (vv. 4–5,11–12) and he bases his appeals on Scripture.

**2:4 *As you come to him.*** Here in verse 4 he pictures them coming to the Lord—though he changes his metaphor. Now Jesus is the living Stone. In verse 5 he tells them what will happen as they come: they will become a spiritual house in which they serve God as a holy priesthood. "The phrase 'as you come to him' expresses the idea of drawing near with intention both to stay and to enjoy personal fellowship" (Stibbs). This verb is used in the Old Testament for coming to God in worship.

***the living Stone.*** Peter shifts his description of Jesus from the "lamb without blemish" (1:19) to "the living Stone." He gets this metaphor from two Old Testament texts: Isaiah 28:16 (v. 6) speaks of "a chosen and precious cornerstone" and Psalm 118:22 (v. 7) speaks of the rejection of that stone. Both verses point out the supreme value of the cornerstone. Peter's point is that, despite his rejection, Christ is the chosen one of God, and in the end he prevails.

***living.*** An allusion to Christ's resurrection (see 1:3,21). He is alive and able to give his resurrection life to those who come to him.

***chosen.*** Peter has already made the point that they have been chosen by God (see notes for 1:2) and he will make the same point again (see v. 9). Here he adds to this the fact that Jesus was also chosen by God. Furthermore, this fact was not accepted. People rejected Jesus. In like manner, this will be their experience; they will be chosen but rejected.

***precious.*** People may reject Jesus, but God gives him great honor.

**2:5 *you also, like living stones.*** So close is the relationship between Christians and Christ that Peter uses the same metaphor to describe both. The implication is that these Christians (like Christ) will know rejection and triumph.

***being built into.*** Stones by themselves serve no function. But shaped together into a structure by a master builder, they become something of use and importance.

***a spiritual house.*** Peter shifts from a biological image ("newborn babies"—2:2) to an architectural one. They are a "spiritual house." As living stones they have been built into a holy temple. The church is the temple of God, made up of a close-knit community of men and women. Here is where God dwells, in contrast to temples built by human hands.

> *The church is the temple of God, made up of a close-knit community of men and women. Here is where God dwells, in contrast to temples built by human hands.*

***a holy priesthood.*** Peter shifts the metaphor again. Not only are they a "spiritual house," they are the priests who serve in it! Priests were common figures in the first-century world. Their function was to mediate between God and the people. Typically, they were members of a special caste; priests were privileged and set apart. But no such elitism exists in the church. All Christians are members of this royal priesthood.

***offering spiritual sacrifices.*** The function of priests was to offer sacrifices of animals, grain, wine, etc. The sacrifice of Christians, however, is spiritual, not material, because Christ's great sacrifice of himself for the sins of the world was the ultimate and final sacrifice. What these New Testament priests can offer to God is love, faith, surrender, service, prayer, thanksgiving, sharing, etc. They offer lives that bring praise (see Rom. 12:1; Eph. 5:1–2; Phil. 4:18; Heb. 13:15–16). Their sacrifice is also "spiritual" in the sense that it is inspired by the Spirit.

**acceptable to God through Jesus Christ.** All their efforts, however, would fail to satisfy God were it not for the sacrifice already made by Jesus himself.

**2:6** In its original context, Isaiah was speaking to the leaders of Israel who had just made a pact with Egypt, in response to the threat of an invasion by Assyria. Isaiah points to the solid temple as an illustration of where their true strength lies. They need to trust God, not alliances. Later, rabbis understood this reference to the cornerstone to be a description of the Messiah whom God would establish in Zion.

> **Christ is the chosen one of God, and in the end he prevails.**

**2:7** In Psalm 118:22, the stone stood for Israel, which the world powers considered useless and which they threw away. However, God gave Israel the most important place in building his kingdom. This text was taken by the early church to be a prophecy of Jesus' rejection and death by the powers-that-be and his subsequent vindication by God as demonstrated in his resurrection and glorification (Acts 4:8–12). This interpretation came from Jesus, who spoke about himself in these terms (Mark 12:10).

**2:8 disobey.** Just as Peter's readers are characterized by their "obedience to Jesus Christ" (1:2), others are characterized by disobedience.

**destined for.** Those who have obeyed are chosen and destined for a glorious inheritance. Those who have stumbled over Christ have a different destiny.

**2:9–10** In contrast to the destiny of their persecutors, they have a fine destiny. Peter lists a series of titles drawn from the Old Testament (primarily from Ex. 19:5–6 and Isa. 43:20–21) which once were applied to Israel, but now belong to them.

**2:9 a chosen people.** Just as Jesus is "chosen by God" (v. 4), so too are they as his people (see also 1:1–2).

**a holy nation.** The church is the true Israel, the heir of all the promises and privileges of the old Israel. The church is not holy "in the sense that either it or its members are in actual fact paragons of virtue, but because it has been set apart for God's service and is inspired and sustained by His Spirit" (Kelly).

**a people belonging to God.** The church is a community chosen by God.

**that you may declare the praises of him.** This is their role. This is what their "spiritual sacrifices" are all about: they are to make God known in the world. In verses 11–12 he spells out what this means.

**2:10** Peter contrasts what they have become with what they once were. This time he draws his language from Hosea (see Hos. 1:6,9; 2:23). The names applied to these Christians are the names God directed Hosea to give to the children born of Gomer.

**2:11 aliens and strangers.** They may be a chosen nation and a royal priesthood, but they are also outsiders in terms of the world in which they live.

**abstain from sinful desires.** "Sinful desires" is literally "fleshly lusts." It is translated as it is here in order to convey its real meaning since "fleshly lusts" is a phrase that has come to stand for sexual sin. However, in the New Testament sins of the flesh encompass a far wider sphere than sexuality, including such things as pride, envy, hatred, etc. (see Gal. 5:19–21 for a representative list).

# 5 Submit Yourselves—1 Peter 2:13–25

## THREE-PART AGENDA

**ICE-BREAKER**
15 Minutes

**BIBLE STUDY**
30 Minutes

**CARING TIME**
15–45 Minutes

> **LEADER: Have you started working with your group about your mission—for instance, by having them review pages M3 and M6 in the center section? If you have a new person at the meeting, remember to do an appropriate ice-breaker from the center section.**

## TO BEGIN THE BIBLE STUDY TIME
(Choose 1 or 2)

1. In your first "real job," who was your boss? What were they like?

2. As a teenager, what authority figure did you have the most run-ins with?

3. How do you feel about the taxes withheld from your paycheck?

## READ SCRIPTURE & DISCUSS
(If you don't have time for all the questions in this section, conclude the Bible Study [30 min.] by answering question #7.)

1. When you are wronged, are you more likely to let it go, fight for your rights or get even?

2. How are Christians to act toward governmental authority (vv. 13–17)? Why?

3. What does Peter mean by "Submit yourselves" (v. 13)? When it comes to submitting to authority, where do you "draw the line"?

### Submission to Rulers and Masters

*13Submit yourselves for the Lord's sake to every authority instituted among men: whether to the king, as the supreme authority, 14or to governors, who are sent by him to punish those who do wrong and to commend those who do right. 15For it is God's will that by doing good you should silence the ignorant talk of foolish men. 16Live as free men, but do not use your freedom as a cover-up for evil; live as servants of God. 17Show proper respect to everyone: Love the brotherhood of believers, fear God, honor the king.*

*18Slaves, submit yourselves to your masters with all respect, not only to those who are good and considerate, but also to those who are harsh. 19For it is commendable if a man bears up under the pain of unjust suffering because he is conscious of God. 20But how is it to your credit if you receive a beating for doing wrong and endure it? But if you suffer for doing good and you endure it, this is commendable before God. 21To this you were called, because Christ suffered for you, leaving you an example, that you should follow in his steps.*

*22"He committed no sin,*
    *and no deceit was found in his mouth."*a

*23When they hurled their insults at him, he did not retaliate; when he suffered, he made no threats. Instead, he entrusted himself to him who judges justly. 24He himself bore our sins in his body on the tree, so that we might die to sins and live for righteousness; by his wounds you have been healed. 25For you were like sheep going astray, but now you have returned to the Shepherd and Overseer of your souls.*

a22 Isaiah 53:9

4. In relation to suffering, verse 21 says, "To this you were called." What is your reaction to this?

5. How can Christ's example (vv. 21–23) help you when you are mistreated? Beyond his example, what benefits has Christ's suffering produced (vv. 24–25)?

6. Who are some of the authority figures in your life? How well are you relating to them? What can you do to improve?

7. To whom do you need to submit yourself more fully to this week? In what way can you do this?

## CARING TIME

(Choose 1 or 2 of these questions before closing in prayer. Be sure to pray for the empty chair.)

1. What is your dream for the future mission of this group?

2. It's not too late to have someone new come to this group. Who can you invite for next week?

3. How can the group remember you in prayer this week?

**Summary.** In the first part of his letter, Peter deals with the *identity* of the people of God (1:1–2:12). In the second part, which begins with this passage, he looks at the *responsibilities* of the people of God (2:13–4:11). Here in this section, he begins his discussion of lifestyle by counseling them to adopt an attitude of respect. He starts by urging respect for everyone (vv. 13–17), with a special look at civil authorities. He then goes on to urge slaves to respect their masters (vv. 18–25).

**2:13–17** Peter begins by counseling respect for all people. Although special attention is focused on rulers, the call is general in nature: "Show proper respect to everyone" (v. 17). They are to do this "for the Lord's sake" (v. 13) because they are the "servants of God" (v. 16).

**2:13 *Submit yourselves.*** This is the key concept in the next two passages. What Peter urges is voluntary subordination in all spheres of human life. When the verb "submit" is used in the New Testament, it is voluntary in nature (e.g., "submit yourself"). The call is never to make others submit to you. They are to "yield to," "adapt to," "give way to" others. In other words, "the principle of the redeemed Christian life must not be self-assertion or mutual exploitation, but the voluntary subordination of oneself to others (see also Rom. 12:10; Eph. 5:21; Phil. 2:3)" (Kelly).

**to every authority instituted among men.** This phrase literally means "every human creature." In fact, the Greek word *ktisei* (translated "authority" in the NIV) "so far from meaning 'institution,' 'ordinance' or 'authority,' ... always in the Bible signifies 'creation' or, concretely, 'creature'" (Kelly). Understanding the phrase this way reinforces the generalized nature of this call which is spelled out clearly in verse 17: "Show proper respect to everyone."

**2:13–14 *king / governors.*** This first situation in which Peter applies this general principle is with civil authorities. Peter's instructions here are quite similar to those of Paul in Romans 13:1–7 and Jesus in Matthew 22:21. The New Testament counsels Christians to be model citizens of the country they inhabit.

**2:14 *punish / commend.*** The role of these authorities is to prevent crime and suppress injustice. How they "commend those who do right" is not clear, though what Peter may mean by this is that governments tend to look with favor on law-abiding citizens (which is what Peter is urging these Asian Christians to be).

**2:15** These Christians were, apparently, subject to slander ("ignorant talk") on the part of people who did not really know what was going on ("foolish men").

***ignorant talk.*** The Greek word used here suggests willful ignorance; the unwillingness to find out what is really true.

**2:16** Christ brought new freedom to men and women who had been long bound by rules and regulations. While affirming this newfound freedom, Peter cautions that they must not let their liberty degenerate into license.

***live as servants of God.*** The paradox is that Christians are both free and bound. They are to "live as free men" while simultaneously they are "slaves of God" ("servants" is literally "slaves").

> *What Peter urges is voluntary subordination in all spheres of human life. When the verb "submit" is used in the New Testament, it is voluntary in nature (e.g., "submit yourself"). The call is never to make others submit to you. They are to "yield to," "adapt to," "give way to" others. In other words, "the principle of the redeemed Christian life must not be self-assertion or mutual exploitation, but the voluntary subordination of oneself to others."*

**2:17** Peter gives two pairs of commands here. The inclusiveness of "everyone" is balanced by the more focused concern for the "brotherhood." Likewise, the local authority of the king is set in the context of the overarching authority of God.

# Leadership Training Supplement

YOU ARE
HERE

| BIRTH | GROWTH | DEVELOP | REBIRTH |
|:---:|:---:|:---:|:---:|
| 101 | 201 | 301 | 401 |

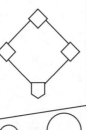
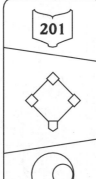
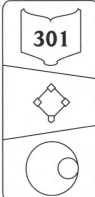
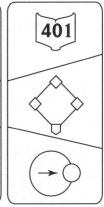

# What is the game plan for your group in the 201 stage?

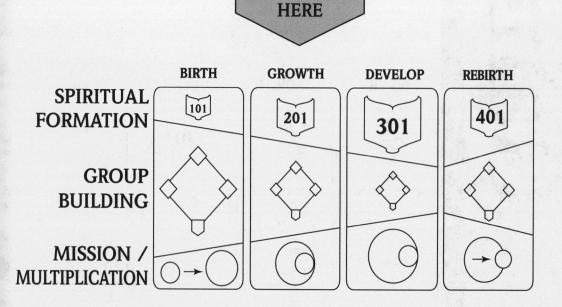

YOU ARE
HERE

| | BIRTH | GROWTH | DEVELOP | REBIRTH |
|---|---|---|---|---|
| SPIRITUAL FORMATION | 101 | 201 | 301 | 401 |
| GROUP BUILDING | | | | |
| MISSION / MULTIPLICATION | | | | |

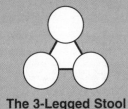

**The 3-Legged Stool**

The three essentials in a healthy small group are Bible Study, Group Building and Mission / Multiplication. You need all three to stay balanced—like a 3-legged stool.

- To focus only on Bible Study will lead to scholasticism.
- To focus only on Group Building will lead to narcissism.
- To focus only on Mission will lead to burnout.

You need a game plan for the life cycle of the group where all of these elements are present in a purpose-driven strategy:

# Spiritual Formation (Bible Study)

**To dig into Scripture as a group.**

Group Bible Study is quite different from individual Bible Study. The guided discussion questions are open-ended. And for those with little Bible background, there are reference notes to bring their knowledge level up so they do not feel intimidated. This helps level the playing field.

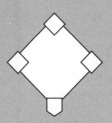

# Group Building

**To transform your group into a mission-driven team.**

The nine basic needs of a group will be assigned to nine different people. Everyone has a job to fill, and when everyone is doing their job the group will grow spiritually and numerically. When new people enter the group, there is a selection of ICE-BREAKERS to start off the meeting and let the new people get acquainted.

# Mission / Multiplication

**To identify the Apprentice / Leader for birthing a new group.**

In this stage, you will start dreaming about the possibility of starting a new group down the road. The questions at the close of each session will lead you carefully through the dreaming process—to help you discover an Apprentice / Leader who will eventually be the leader of a new group. This is an exciting challenge! (See page M6 for more about Mission / Multiplication.)

## Bible Study

**What is unique about Serendipity Group Bible Study?**

Bible Study for groups is based on six principles. Principle 1: Level the playing field so that everyone can share—those who know the Bible and those who do not know the Bible. Principle 2: Share your spiritual story and let the people in your group get to know you. Principle 3: Ask open-ended questions that have no right or wrong answers. Principle 4: Use the 3-part agenda. Principle 5: Subdivide into smaller subgroups so that everyone can partici-pate. Principle 6: Affirm One Another—"Thanks for sharing."

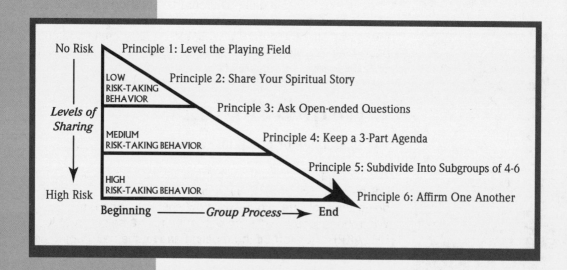

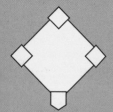

## Group Building

**What are the jobs that are needed on your team roster?**

In the first or second session of this course, you need to fill out the roster on the next page. Then check every few weeks to see that everyone is "playing their position." If you do not have nine people in your group, you can double up on jobs until new peo-ple join your group and are assigned a job. The goal is to field a team. Building a team will better prepare you to rebirth a new group when the group becomes pregnant.

## Your Small Group Team Roster

**Mission Leader**
(Left Field)
Keeps group focused on the mission to invite new people and eventually give birth to a new group. This person needs to be passionate and have a long-term perspective.

_____

**Host**
(Center Field)
Environmental engineer in charge of meeting location. Always on the lookout for moving to a new meeting location where new people will feel the "home field advantage."

_____

**Party Leader**
(Right Field)
Designates who is going to bring refreshments. Plans a party every month or so where new people are invited to visit and children are welcome.

_____

**Caretaker**
(Shortstop)
Takes new members under their wing. Makes sure they get acquainted. Always has an extra book, name tags and a list of group members and phone numbers.

_____

**Bible Study Leader**
(Second Base)
Takes over in the Bible Study time (30 minutes). Follows the agenda. Keeps the group moving. This person must be very time-conscious.

_____

**Group Leader**
(Pitcher)
Puts ball in play. Team encourager. Motivator. Sees to it that everyone is involved in the team effort.

_____

**Caring Time Leader**
(Third Base)
Takes over in the Caring Time. Records prayer requests and follows up on any prayer needs during the week. This person is the "heart" of the group.

_____

**Worship Leader**
(First Base)
Leads the group in singing and prayer when it is appropriate. Also leads the icebreaker to get acquainted, before the opening prayer.

_____

**Apprentice / Leader**
(Catcher)
The other half of the battery. Observes the infield. Calls "time" to discuss strategy and regroup. Stays focused.

_____

# Mission / Multiplication

**Where are you in the 4-stage life cycle of your mission?**

You can't sit on a one-legged stool—or even a two-legged stool. It takes all three. The same is true of a small group; you need all three legs. A Bible Study and Care Group will eventually fall if it does not have a mission.

The mission goal is to eventually give birth to a new group. In this 201 course, the goals are: 1) to keep inviting new people to join your group and 2) to discover the Apprentice / Leader and leadership core for starting a new group down the road.

When a new person comes to the group, start off the meeting with one of the ice-breakers on the following pages. These ice-breakers are designed to be fun and easy to share, but they have a very important purpose—that is, to let the new person get acquainted with the group and share their spiritual story with the group, and hear the spiritual stories of those in the group.

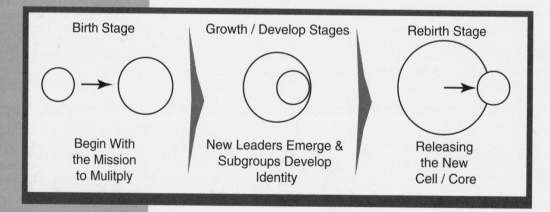

| Birth Stage | Growth / Develop Stages | Rebirth Stage |
| --- | --- | --- |
| Begin With the Mission to Mulitply | New Leaders Emerge & Subgroups Develop Identity | Releasing the New Cell / Core |

# Ice-Breakers

# I Am Somebody Who ...

Rotate around the group, one person reading the first item, the next person reading the second item, etc. Before answering, let everyone in the group try to GUESS what the answer would be: "Yes" ... "No" ... or "Maybe." After everyone has guessed, explain the answer. Anyone who guessed right gets $10. When every item on the list has been read, the person with the most "money" WINS.

I AM SOMEBODY WHO ...

**Y N M**
- ☐ ☐ ☐ would go on a blind date
- ☐ ☐ ☐ sings in the shower
- ☐ ☐ ☐ listens to music full blast
- ☐ ☐ ☐ likes to dance
- ☐ ☐ ☐ cries at movies
- ☐ ☐ ☐ stops to smell the flowers
- ☐ ☐ ☐ daydreams a lot
- ☐ ☐ ☐ likes to play practical jokes
- ☐ ☐ ☐ makes a "to do" list
- ☐ ☐ ☐ loves liver
- ☐ ☐ ☐ won't use a portable toilet
- ☐ ☐ ☐ likes thunderstorms
- ☐ ☐ ☐ enjoys romance novels
- ☐ ☐ ☐ loves crossword puzzles
- ☐ ☐ ☐ hates flying
- ☐ ☐ ☐ fixes my own car

**Y N M**
- ☐ ☐ ☐ would enjoy skydiving
- ☐ ☐ ☐ has a black belt in karate
- ☐ ☐ ☐ watches soap operas
- ☐ ☐ ☐ is afraid of the dark
- ☐ ☐ ☐ goes to bed early
- ☐ ☐ ☐ plays the guitar
- ☐ ☐ ☐ talks to plants
- ☐ ☐ ☐ will ask a stranger for directions
- ☐ ☐ ☐ sleeps until the last second
- ☐ ☐ ☐ likes to travel alone
- ☐ ☐ ☐ reads the financial page
- ☐ ☐ ☐ saves for a rainy day
- ☐ ☐ ☐ lies about my age
- ☐ ☐ ☐ yells at the umpire
- ☐ ☐ ☐ closes my eyes during scary movies

# Press Conference

This is a great activity for a new group or when new people are joining an established group. Interview one person with these questions.

1. What is your nickname and how did you get it?

2. Where did you grow up? Where was the "watering hole" in your hometown—where kids got together?

3. What did you do for kicks then? What about now?

4. What was the turning point in your spiritual life?

5. What prompted you to come to this group?

6. What do you want to get out of this group?

# Down Memory Lane

Celebrate the childhood memories of the way you were. Choose one or more of the topics listed below and take turns answering the question related to it. If time allows, do another round.

HOME SWEET HOME–What do you remember about your childhood home?

TELEVISION—What was your favorite TV program or radio show?

OLD SCHOOLHOUSE—What were your best and worst subjects in school?

LIBRARY—What did you like to read (and where)?

TELEPHONE—How much time did you spend on the phone each day?

MOVIES—Who was your favorite movie star?

CASH FLOW—What did you do for spending money?

SPORTS—What was your favorite sport or team?

GRANDPA'S HOUSE—Where did your grandparents live? When did you visit them?

POLICE—Did you ever get in trouble with the law?

WEEKENDS—What was the thing to do on Saturday night?


# Wallet Scavenger Hunt

With your wallet or purse, use the set of questions below. You get two minutes in silence to go through your possessions and find these items. Then break the silence and "show-and-tell" what you have chosen. For instance, "The thing I have had for the longest time is ... this picture of me when I was a baby."

1. The thing I have had for the LONGEST TIME in my wallet is ...

2. The thing that has SENTIMENTAL VALUE is ...

3. The thing that reminds me of a FUN TIME is ...

4. The most REVEALING thing about me in my wallet is ...

# The Grand Total

This is a fun ice-breaker that has additional uses. You can use this ice-breaker to divide your group into two subgroups (odds and evens). You can also calculate who has the highest and lowest totals if you need a fun way to select someone to do a particular task, such as bring refreshments or be first to tell their story.

Fill each box with the correct number and then total your score. When everyone is finished, go around the group and explain how you got your total.

|  |  |  |  |  |
|---|---|---|---|---|
| ☐ | X | ☐ | = | ☐ |
| Number of hours you sleep | | Number of miles you walk daily | | Subtotal |
| ☐ | — | ☐ | = | ☐ |
| Number of speeding tickets you've received | | Number of times sent to principal's office | | Subtotal |
| ☐ | ÷ | ☐ | = | ☐ |
| Number of hours spent watching TV daily | | Number of books you read this year for fun | | Subtotal |
| ☐ | + | ☐ | = | ☐ |
| Number of push-ups you can do | | Number of pounds you lost this year | | Subtotal |

☐

GRAND
TOTAL

# Find Yourself in the Picture

In this drawing, which child do you identify with—or which one best portrays you right now? Share with your group which child you would choose and why. You can also use this as an affirmation exercise, by assigning each person in your group to a child in the picture.

# Four Facts, One Lie

Everyone in the group should answer the following five questions. One of the five answers should be a lie! The rest of the group members can guess which of your answers is a lie.

1.  At age 7, my favorite TV show was ...

2.  At age 9, my hero was ...

3.  At age 11, I wanted to be a ...

4.  At age 13, my favorite music was ...

5.  Right now, my favorite pastime is ...

# Old-Fashioned Auction

Just like an old-fashioned auction, conduct an out loud auction in your group—starting each item at $50. Everybody starts out with $1,000. Select an auctioneer. This person can also get in on the bidding. Remember, start the bidding on each item at $50. Then, write the winning bid in the left column and the winner's name in the right column. Remember, you only have $1,000 to spend for the whole game. AUCTIONEER: Start off by asking, "Who will give me $50 for a 1965 red MG convertible?" ... and keep going until you have a winner. Keep this auction to 10 minutes.

WINNING BID                                                                 WINNER

$_____  1965 red MG convertible in perfect condition        _____

$_____  Winter vacation in Hawaii for two                   _____

$_____  Two Super Bowl tickets on the 50-yard line          _____

$_____  One year of no hassles with my kids / parents       _____

$_____  Holy Land tour hosted by my favorite Christian      _____
                  leader

$_____  Season pass to ski resort of my choice              _____

$_____  Two months off to do anything I want, with pay      _____

$_____  Home theater with surround sound                    _____

$_____  Breakfast in bed for one year                       _____

$_____  Two front-row tickets at the concert of my choice _____

$_____  Two-week Caribbean cruise with my spouse in         _____
                  honeymoon suite

$_____  Shopping spree at Saks Fifth Avenue                 _____

$_____  Six months of maid service                         _____

$_____  All-expense-paid family vacation to Disney World_____

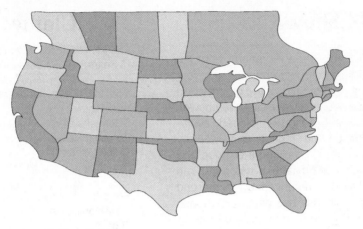

# Places in My Life

On the map above, put six dots to indicate these significant places in your journey. Then go around and have each person explain the dots:

- the place where I was born
- the place where I spent most of my life
- the place where I first fell in love
- the place where I went or would like to go on a vacation
- the place where God first became real to me
- the place where I would like to retire

# The Four Quaker Questions

This is an old Quaker activity which Serendipity has adapted over the years. Go around the group and share your answers to the questions, everyone answering #1. Then, everyone answers #2, etc. This ice-breaker has been known to take between 30 and 60 minutes for some groups.

1. Where were you living between the ages of 7 and 12, and what were the winters like then?

2. How was your home heated during that time?

3. What was the center of warmth in your life when you were a child? (It could be a place in the house, a time of year, a person, etc.)

4. When did God become a "warm" person to you ... and how did it happen?

# KWIZ Show

Like a TV quiz show, someone from the group picks a category and reads the four questions—pausing to let the others in the group guess before revealing the answer. When the first person is finished, everyone adds up the money they won by guessing right. Go around the group and have each person take a category. The person with the most money at the end wins. To begin, ask one person to choose a CATEGORY and read out loud the $1 question. Before answering, let everyone try to GUESS the answer. When everyone has guessed, the person answers the question, and anyone who guessed right puts $1 in the margin, etc. until the first person has read all four questions in the CATEGORY.

# Clothes

**For $1:** I'm more likely to shop at:
❏ Sears        ❏ Saks Fifth Avenue

**For $2:** I feel more comfortable wearing:
❏ formal clothes
❏ casual clothes
❏ sport clothes
❏ grubbies

**For $3:** In buying clothes, I look for:
❏ fashion / style
❏ price
❏ name brand
❏ quality

**For $4:** In buying clothes, I usually:
❏ shop all day for a bargain
❏ go to one store, but try on everything
❏ buy the first thing I try on
❏ buy without trying it on

# Tastes

**For $1:** In music, I am closer to:
❏ Bach        ❏ Beatles

**For $2:** In furniture, I prefer:
❏ Early American
❏ French Provincial
❏ Scandinavian—contemporary
❏ Hodgepodge—little of everything

**For $3:** My favorite choice of reading material is:
❏ science fiction    ❏ sports
❏ mystery            ❏ romance

**For $4:** If I had $1,000 to splurge, I would buy:
❏ one original painting
❏ two numbered prints
❏ three reproductions and an easy chair
❏ four cheap imitations, an easy chair and a color TV

# Travel

**For $1:** For travel, I prefer:
❏ excitement        ❏ enrichment

**For $2:** On a vacation, my lifestyle is:
❏ go-go all the time
❏ slow and easy
❏ party every night and sleep in

**For $3:** In packing for a trip, I include:
❏ toothbrush and change of underwear
❏ light bag and good book
❏ small suitcase and nice outfit
❏ all but the kitchen sink

**For $4:** If I had money to blow, I would choose:
❏ one glorious night in a luxury hotel
❏ a weekend in a nice hotel
❏ a full week in a cheap motel
❏ two weeks camping in the boon-docks

# Habits

**For $1:** I am more likely to squeeze the toothpaste:
- ❐ in the middle   ❐ from the end

**For $2:** If I am lost, I will probably:
- ❐ stop and ask directions
- ❐ check the map
- ❐ find the way by driving around

**For $3:** I read the newspaper starting with the:
- ❐ front page
- ❐ funnies
- ❐ sports
- ❐ entertainment section

**For $4:** When I get ready for bed, I put my clothes:
- ❐ on a hanger in the closet
- ❐ folded neatly over a chair
- ❐ into a hamper or clothes basket
- ❐ on the floor

# Shows

**For $1:** I am more likely to:
- ❐ go see a first-run movie
- ❐ rent a video at home

**For $2:** On TV, my first choice is:
- ❐ news
- ❐ sports
- ❐ sitcoms

**For $3:** If a show gets too scary, I will usually:
- ❐ go to the restroom
- ❐ close my eyes
- ❐ clutch a friend
- ❐ love it

**For $4:** In movies, I prefer:
- ❐ romantic comedies
- ❐ serious drama
- ❐ action films
- ❐ Disney animation

# Food

**For $1:** I prefer to eat at a:
- ❐ fast-food restaurant
- ❐ fancy restaurant

**For $2:** On the menu, I look for something:
- ❐ familiar
- ❐ different
- ❐ way-out

**For $3:** When eating chicken, my preference is a:
- ❐ drumstick
- ❐ wing
- ❐ breast
- ❐ gizzard

**For $4:** I draw the line when it comes to eating:
- ❐ frog legs
- ❐ snails
- ❐ raw oysters
- ❐ Rocky Mountain oysters

# Work

**For $1:** I prefer to work at a job that is:
- ❐ too big to handle
- ❐ too small to be challenging

**For $2:** The job I find most unpleasant to do is:
- ❐ cleaning the house
- ❐ working in the yard
- ❐ balancing the checkbook

**For $3:** In choosing a job, I look for:
- ❐ salary
- ❐ security
- ❐ fulfillment
- ❐ working conditions

**For $4:** If I had to choose between these jobs, I would choose:
- ❐ pickle inspector at processing plant
- ❐ complaint officer at department store
- ❐ bedpan changer at hospital
- ❐ personnel manager in charge of firing

# Let Me Tell You About My Day

What was your day like today? Use one of the characters below to help you describe your day to the group. Feel free to elaborate.

**GREEK TRAGEDY**
It was classic, not a dry eye
in the house.

**EPISODE OF
THREE STOOGES**
I was Larry, trapped
between Curly and Moe.

**SOAP OPERA**
I didn't think these
things could happen,
until it happened to me.

**ACTION ADVENTURE**
When I rode onto the
scene, everybody noticed.

**BIBLE EPIC**
Cecil B. DeMille couldn't
have done it any better.

**LATE NIGHT NEWS**
It might as well have
been broadcast over the
airwaves.

**BORING LECTURE**
The biggest
challenge of the day was
staying awake.

**PROFESSIONAL WRESTLING MATCH**
I feel as if Hulk Hogan's been coming after me.

**FIREWORKS DISPLAY**
It was spectacular.

# Music in My Life

Put an *"X"* on the first line below—somewhere between the two extremes—to indicate how you are feeling right now. Share your answers, and then repeat this process down the list. If you feel comfortable, briefly explain your response.

IN MY PERSONAL LIFE, I'M FEELING LIKE ...
**Blues in the Night**_____ **Feeling Groovy**

IN MY FAMILY LIFE, I'M FEELING LIKE ...
**Stormy Weather** _____ **The Sound of Music**

IN MY EMOTIONAL LIFE, I'M FEELING LIKE ...
**The Feeling Is Gone** _____ **On Eagle's Wings**

IN MY WORK, SCHOOL OR CAREER, I'M FEELING LIKE ...
**Take This Job and Shove It** _____ **The Future's So Bright I Gotta Wear Shades**

IN MY SPIRITUAL LIFE, I'M FEELING LIKE ...
**Sounds of Silence** _____ **Hallelujah Chorus**

# My Childhood Table

Try to recall the table where you ate most of your meals as a child, and the people who sat around that table. Use the questions below to describe these significant relationships, and how they helped to shape the person you are today.

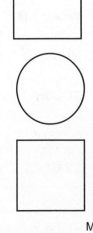

1. What was the shape of the table?
2. Where did you sit?
3. Who else was at the table?
4. If you had to describe each person with a color, what would be the color of (for instance):
   ☐ Your father? (e.g., dark blue, because he was conservative like IBM)
   ☐ Your mother? (e.g., light green, because she reminded me of springtime)
5. If you had to describe the atmosphere at the table with a color, what would you choose? (e.g., bright orange, because it was warm and light)
6. Who was the person at the table who praised you and made you feel special?
7. Who provided the spiritual leadership in your home?

# Home Improvement

Take inventory of your own life. Bob Munger, in his booklet *My Heart—Christ's Home*, describes the areas of a person's life as the rooms of a house. Give yourself a grade on each room as follows, then share with the others your best and worst grade.

- ❐ A = excellent
- ❐ B = good
- ❐ C = passing, needs a little dusting
- ❐ D = passing, but needs a lot of improvement

LIBRARY: This room is in your mind—what you allow to go into it and come out of it. It is the "control room" of the entire house.

DINING ROOM: Appetites, desires; those things your mind and spirit feed on for nourishment.

DRAWING ROOM: This is where you draw close to God—seeking time with him daily, not just in times of distress or need.

WORKSHOP: This room is where your gifts, talents and skills are put to work for God—by the power of the Spirit.

RUMPUS ROOM: The social area of your life; the things you do to amuse yourself and others.

HALL CLOSET: The one secret place that no one knows about, but is a real stumbling block in your walk in the Spirit.

# How Is It With Your Soul?

John Wesley, the founder of the Methodist Church, asked his "class meetings" to check in each week at their small group meeting with this question: "How is it with your soul?" To answer this question, choose one of these four allegories to explain the past week in your life:

WEATHER: For example: "This week has been mostly cloudy, with some thunderstorms at midweek. Right now, the weather is a little brighter ..."

MUSIC: For example: "This past week has been like heavy rock music—almost too loud. The sound seems to reverberate off the walls."

COLOR: For example: "This past week has been mostly fall colors—deep orange, flaming red and pumpkin."

SEASON OF THE YEAR: For example: "This past week has been like springtime. New signs of life are beginning to appear on the barren trees, and a few shoots of winter wheat are breaking through the frozen ground."

# My Spiritual Journey

The half-finished sentences below are designed to help you share your spiritual story. Ask one person to finish all the sentences. Then move to the next person, etc. If you are short on time, have only one person tell their story in this session.

1. RELIGIOUS BACKGROUND: My spiritual story begins in my home as a child, where the religious training was ...

2. CHURCH: The church that I went to as a child was ...

3. SIGNIFICANT PERSON: The person who had the greatest influence on my spiritual formation was ...

4. PERSONAL ENCOUNTER: The first time God became more than just a name to me was when ...

5. JOURNEY: Since my personal encounter with God, my Christian life might be described as ...

6. PRESENT: On a scale from 1 to 10, I would describe my spiritual energy level right now as a ...

7. NEXT STEP: The thing I need to work on right now in my spiritual life is ...

# Bragging Rights

Check your group for bragging rights in these categories.

❏ SPEEDING TICKETS: the person with the most speeding tickets
❏ BROKEN BONES: the person with the most broken bones
❏ STITCHES: the person with the most stitches
❏ SCARS: the person with the longest scar
❏ FISH OR GAME: the person who claims they caught the largest fish or killed the largest animal
❏ STUNTS: the person with the most death-defying story
❏ IRON: the person who can pump the most iron

# Personal Habits

Have everyone in your group finish the sentence on the first category by putting an "*X*" somewhere between the two extremes (e.g., on HOUSEWORK ... I would put myself closer to "Where's the floor?"). Repeat this process down the list as time permits.

ON HOUSEWORK, I AM SOMEWHERE BETWEEN:
Eat off the floor_____Where's the floor?

ON COOKING, I AM SOMEWHERE BETWEEN:
Every meal is an act of worship_____Make it fast and hold the frills

ON EXERCISING, I AM SOMEWHERE BETWEEN:
Workout every morning_____Click the remote

ON SHOPPING, I AM SOMEWHERE BETWEEN:
Shop all day for a bargain_____Only the best

ON EATING, I AM SOMEWHERE BETWEEN:
You are what you eat_____Eat, drink and be merry

# American Graffiti

If Hollywood made a movie about your life on the night of your high school prom, what would be needed? Let each person in your group have a few minutes to recall these details. If you have more than four or five in your group, ask everyone to choose two or three topics to talk about.

1. LOCATION: Where were you living?
2. WEIGHT: How much did you weigh—soaking wet?
3. PROM: Where was it held?
4. DATE: Who did you go with?
5. CAR / TRANSPORTATION: How did you get there?
   (If you used a car, what was the model, year, color, condition?)
6. ATTIRE: What did you wear?
7. PROGRAM: What was the entertainment?
8. AFTERWARD: What did you do afterward?
9. HIGHLIGHT: What was the highlight of the evening?
10. HOMECOMING: If you could go back and visit your high school, who would you like to see?

# Group Orchestra

Read out loud the first item and let everyone nominate the person in your group for this musical instrument in your group orchestra. Then, read aloud the next instrument, and call out another name, etc.

ANGELIC HARP: Soft, gentle, melodious, wooing with heavenly sounds.

OLD-FASHIONED WASHBOARD: Nonconforming, childlike and fun.

PLAYER PIANO: Mischievous, raucous, honky-tonk—delightfully carefree.

KETTLEDRUM: Strong, vibrant, commanding when needed but usually in the background.

PASSIONATE CASTANET: Full of Spanish fervor—intense and always upbeat.

STRADIVARIUS VIOLIN: Priceless, exquisite, soul-piercing—with the touch of the master.

FLUTTERING FLUTE: Tender, lighthearted, wide-ranging and clear as crystal.

SCOTTISH BAGPIPES: Forthright, distinctive and unmistakable.

SQUARE DANCE FIDDLE: Folksy, down-to-earth, toe-tapping—sprightly and full of energy.

ENCHANTING OBOE: Haunting, charming, disarming—even the cobra is harmless with this sound.

MELLOW CELLO: Deep, sonorous, compassionate—adding body and depth to the orchestra.

PIPE ORGAN: Grand, magnificent, rich—versatile and commanding.

HERALDING TRUMPET: Stirring, lively, invigorating—signaling attention and attack.

CLASSICAL GUITAR: Contemplative, profound, thoughtful *and* thought-provoking.

ONE-MAN BAND: Able to do many things well, all at once.

COMB AND TISSUE PAPER: Makeshift, original, uncomplicated—homespun and creative.

SWINGING TROMBONE: Warm, rich—great in solo or background support.

# Broadway Show

Imagine for a moment that your group has been chosen to produce a Broadway show, and you have to choose people from your group for all of the jobs for this production. Have someone read out loud the job description for the first job below—PRODUCER. Then, let everyone in your group call out the name of the person in your group who would best fit this job. (You don't have to agree.) Then read the job description for the next job and let everyone nominate another person, etc. You only have 10 minutes for this assignment, so move fast.

PRODUCER: Typical Hollywood business tycoon; extravagant, big-budget, big-production magnate in the Steven Spielberg style.

DIRECTOR: Creative, imaginative brains who coordinates the production and draws the best out of others.

HEROINE: Beautiful, captivating, everybody's heart throb; defenseless when men are around, but nobody's fool.

HERO: Tough, macho, champion of the underdog, knight in shining armor; defender of truth.

COMEDIAN: Childlike, happy-go-lucky, outrageously funny, keeps everyone laughing.

CHARACTER PERSON: Rugged individualist, outrageously different, colorful, adds spice to any surrounding.

FALL GUY: Easy-going, nonchalant character who wins the hearts of everyone by being the "foil" of the heavy characters.

TECHNICAL DIRECTOR: The genius for "sound and lights"; creates the perfect atmosphere.

COMPOSER OF LYRICS: Communicates in music what everybody understands; heavy into feelings, moods, outbursts of energy.

PUBLICITY AGENT: Advertising and public relations expert; knows all the angles, good at one-liners, a flair for "hot" news.

VILLAIN: The "bad guy" who really is the heavy for the plot, forces others to think, challenges traditional values; out to destroy anything artificial or hypocritical.

AUTHOR: Shy, aloof; very much in touch with feelings, sensitive to people, puts into words what others only feel.

STAGEHAND: Supportive, behind-the-scenes person who makes things run smoothly; patient and tolerant.

# Wild Predictions

Try to match the people in your group to the crazy forecasts below. (Don't take it too seriously; it's meant to be fun!) Read out loud the first item and ask everyone to call out the name of the person who is most likely to accomplish this feat. Then, read the next item and ask everyone to make a new prediction, etc.

THE PERSON IN OUR GROUP MOST LIKELY TO ...

Make a million selling Beanie Babies over the Internet

Become famous for designing new attire for sumo wrestlers

Replace Vanna White on *Wheel of Fortune*

Appear on *The Tonight Show* to exhibit an acrobatic talent

Move to a desert island

Discover a new use for underarm deodorant

Succeed David Letterman as host of *The Late Show*

Substitute for John Madden as Fox's football color analyst

Appear on the cover of *Muscle & Fitness Magazine*

Become the newest member of the Spice Girls

Work as a bodyguard for Rush Limbaugh at Feminist convention

Write a best-selling novel based on their love life

Be a dance instructor on a cruise ship for wealthy, well-endowed widows

Win the blue ribbon at the state fair for best Rocky Mountain oyster recipe

Land a job as head librarian for Amazon.com

Be the first woman to win the Indianapolis 500

Open the Clouseau Private Detective Agency

# Career Placements

Read the list of career choices aloud and quickly choose someone in your group for each job—based upon their unique gifts and talents. Have fun!

SPACE ENVIRONMENTAL ENGINEER: in charge of designing the bathrooms on space shuttles

SCHOOL BUS DRIVER: for junior high kids in New York City (earplugs supplied)

WRITER: of an "advice to the lovelorn" column in Hollywood

SUPERVISOR: of a complaint department for a large automobile dealership and service department

ANIMAL PSYCHIATRIST: for French poodles in a fashionable suburb of Paris

RESEARCH SCIENTIST: studying the fertilization patterns of the dodo bird—now extinct

SAFARI GUIDE: in the heart of Africa—for wealthy widows and eccentric bachelors

LITTLE LEAGUE BASEBALL COACH: in Mudville, Illinois—last year's record was 0 and 12

MANAGER: of your local McDonald's during the holiday rush with 210 teenage employees

LIBRARIAN: for the Walt Disney Hall of Fame memorabilia

CHOREOGRAPHER: for the Dallas Cowboys cheerleaders

NURSE'S AIDE: at a home for retired Sumo wrestlers

SECURITY GUARD: crowd control officer at a rock concert

ORGANIZER: of paperwork for Congress

PUBLIC RELATIONS MANAGER: for Dennis Rodman

BODYGUARD: for Rush Limbaugh on a speaking tour of feminist groups

TOY ASSEMBLY PERSON: for a toy store over the holidays

# You and Me, Partner

Think of the people in your group as you read over the list of activities below. If you had to choose someone from your group to be your partner, who would you choose to do these activities with? Jot down each person's name beside the activity. You can use each person's name only once and you have to use everyone's name once—so think it through before you jot down their names. Then, let one person listen to what others chose for them. Then, move to the next person, etc., around your group.

WHO WOULD YOU CHOOSE FOR THE FOLLOWING?

_____ ENDURANCE DANCE CONTEST partner

_____ BOBSLED RACE partner for the Olympics

_____ TRAPEZE ACT partner

_____ MY UNDERSTUDY for my debut in a Broadway musical

_____ BEST MAN or MAID OF HONOR at my wedding

_____ SECRET UNDERCOVER AGENT copartner

_____ BODYGUARD for me when I strike it rich

_____ MOUNTAIN CLIMBING partner in climbing Mt. Everest

_____ ASTRONAUT to fly the space shuttle while I walk in space

_____ SAND CASTLE TOURNAMENT building partner

_____ PIT CREW foreman for entry in Indianapolis 500

_____ AUTHOR for my biography

_____ SURGEON to operate on me for a life-threatening cancer

_____ NEW BUSINESS START-UP partner

_____ TAG-TEAM partner for a professional wrestling match

_____ HEAVY-DUTY PRAYER partner

# My Gourmet Group

Here's a chance to pass out some much deserved praise for the people who have made your group something special. Ask one person to sit in silence while the others explain the delicacy they would choose to describe the contribution this person has made to your group. Repeat the process for each member of the group.

CAVIAR: That special touch of class and aristocratic taste that has made the rest of us feel like royalty.

PRIME RIB: Stable, brawny, macho, the generous mainstay of any menu; juicy, mouth-watering "perfect cut" for good nourishment.

IMPORTED CHEESE: Distinctive, tangy, mellow with age; adds depth to any meal.

VINEGAR AND OIL: Tart, witty, dry; a rare combination of healing ointment and pungent spice to add "bite" to the salad.

ARTICHOKE HEARTS: Tender and disarmingly vulnerable; whets the appetite for heartfelt sharing.

FRENCH PASTRY: Tempting, irresistible "creme de la creme" dessert; the connoisseur's delight for topping off a meal.

PHEASANT UNDER GLASS: Wild, totally unique, a rare dish for people who appreciate original fare.

CARAFE OF WINE: Sparkling, effervescent, exuberant and joyful; outrageously free and liberating to the rest of us.

ESCARGOT AND OYSTERS: Priceless treasures of the sea once out of their shells; succulent, delicate and irreplaceable.

FRESH FRUIT: Vine-ripened, energy-filled, invigorating; the perfect treat after a heavy meal.

ITALIAN ICE CREAMS: Colorful, flavorful, delightfully childlike; the unexpected surprise in our group.

# Thank You

How would you describe your experience with this group? Choose one of the animals below that best describes how your experience in this group affected your life. Then share your responses with the group.

WILD EAGLE: You have helped to heal my wings, and taught me how to soar again.

TOWERING GIRAFFE: You have helped me to hold my head up and stick my neck out, and reach over the fences I have built.

PLAYFUL PORPOISE: You have helped me to find a new freedom and a whole new world to play in.

COLORFUL PEACOCK: You have told me that I'm beautiful; I've started to believe it, and it's changing my life.

SAFARI ELEPHANT: I have enjoyed this new adventure, and I'm not going to forget it, or this group; I can hardly wait for the next safari.

LOVABLE HIPPOPOTAMUS: You have let me surface and bask in the warm sunshine of God's love.

LANKY LEOPARD: You have helped me to look closely at myself and see some spots, and you still accept me the way I am.

DANCING BEAR: You have taught me to dance in the midst of pain, and you have helped me to reach out and hug again.

ALL-WEATHER DUCK: You have helped me to celebrate life—even in stormy weather—and to sing in the rain.

# Academy Awards

You have had a chance to observe the gifts and talents of the members of your group. Now you will have a chance to pass out some much deserved praise for the contribution that each member of the group has made to your life. Read out loud the first award. Then let everyone nominate the person they feel is the most deserving for that award. Then read the next award, etc., through the list. Have fun!

SPARK PLUG AWARD: for the person who ignited the group

DEAR ABBY AWARD: for the person who cared enough to listen

ROYAL GIRDLE AWARD: for the person who supported us

WINNIE THE POOH AWARD: for the warm, caring person when someone needed a hug

ROCK OF GIBRALTER AWARD: for the person who was strong in the tough times of our group

OPRAH AWARD: for the person who asked the fun questions that got us to talk

TED KOPPEL AWARD: for the person who asked the heavy questions that made us think

KING ARTHUR'S AWARD: for the knight in shining armor

PINK PANTHER AWARD: for the detective who made us deal with Scripture

NOBEL PEACE PRIZE: for the person who harmonized our differences of opinion without diminishing anyone

BIG MAC AWARD: for the person who showed the biggest hunger for spiritual things

SERENDIPITY CROWN: for the person who grew the most spiritually during the course—in your estimation

# You Remind Me of Jesus

Every Christian reflects the character of Jesus in some way. As your group has gotten to know each other, you can begin to see how each person demonstrates Christ in their very own personality. Go around the circle and have each person listen while others take turns telling that person what they notice in him or her that reminds them of Jesus. You may also want to tell them why you selected what you did.

YOU REMIND ME OF ...

JESUS THE HEALER: You seem to be able to touch someone's life with your compassion and help make them whole.

JESUS THE SERVANT: There's nothing that you wouldn't do for someone.

JESUS THE PREACHER: You share your faith in a way that challenges and inspires people.

JESUS THE LEADER: As Jesus had a plan for the disciples, you are able to lead others in a way that honors God.

JESUS THE REBEL: By doing the unexpected, you remind me of Jesus' way of revealing God in unique, surprising ways.

JESUS THE RECONCILER: Like Jesus, you have the ability to be a peacemaker between others.

JESUS THE TEACHER: You have a gift for bringing light and understanding to God's Word.

JESUS THE CRITIC: You have the courage to say what needs to be said, even if it isn't always popular.

JESUS THE SACRIFICE: Like Jesus, you seem willing to sacrifice anything to glorify God.

# Reflections

Take some time to evaluate the life of your group by using the statements below. Read the first sentence out loud and ask everyone to explain where they would put a dot between the two extremes. When you are finished, go back and give your group an overall grade in the category of Group Building, Bible Study and Mission.

## GROUP BUILDING

On celebrating life and having fun together, we were more like a ...
wet blanket _____ hot tub

On becoming a caring community, we were more like a ...
prickly porcupine_____cuddly teddy bear

## SPIRITUAL FORMATION (Bible Study)

On sharing our spiritual stories, we were more like a ...
shallow pond _____spring-fed lake

On digging into Scripture, we were more like a ...
slow-moving snail _____voracious anteater

## MISSION

On inviting new people into our group, we were more like a ...
barbed-wire fence _____wide-open door

On stretching our vision for mission, we were more like an ...
ostrich _____eagle

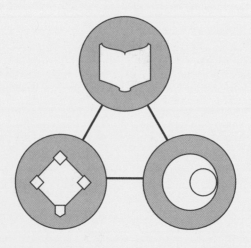

# Human Bingo / Party Mixer

After the leader says "Go!" circulate the room, asking people the things described in the boxes. If someone answers "Yes" to a question, have them sign their initials in that box. Continue until someone completes the entire card—or one row if you don't have that much time. You can only use someone's name twice, and you cannot use your own name on your card.

| | | | | | | |
|---|---|---|---|---|---|---|
| can juggle | TP'd a house | never used an outhouse | sings in the shower | rec'd 6+ traffic tickets | paddled in school | watches Sesame Street |
| sleeps in church regularly | never changed a diaper | split pants in public | milked a cow | born out of the country | has been to Hawaii | can do the splits |
| watches soap operas | can touch tongue to nose | rode a motor-cycle | never ridden a horse | moved twice last year | sleeps on a waterbed | has hole in sock |
| walked in wrong restroom | loves classical music | skipped school | **FREE** | broke a leg | has a hot tub | loves eating sushi |
| is an only child | loves raw oysters | has a 3-inch + scar | doesn't wear PJ's | smoked a cigar | can dance the Charleston | weighs under 110 lbs. |
| likes writing poetry | still has tonsils | loves crossword puzzles | likes bubble baths | wearing Fruit of the Loom | doesn't use mouth-wash | often watches cartoons |
| kissed on first date | can wiggle ears | can play the guitar | plays chess regularly | reads the comics first | can touch palms to floor | sleeps with stuffed animal |

# Group Covenant

Any group can benefit from creating a group covenant. Reserve some time during one of the first meetings to discuss answers to the following questions. When everyone in the group has the same expectations for the group, everything runs more smoothly.

1. The purpose of our group is:

2. The goals of our group are:

3. We will meet for _____ weeks, after which we will decide if we wish to continue as a group. If we do decide to continue, we will reconsider this covenant.

4. We will meet _____ (weekly, every other week, monthly).

5. Our meetings will be from _____ o'clock to _____ o'clock, and we will strive to start and end on time.

6. We will meet at _____ or rotate from house to house.

7. We will take care of the following details:   ❐ child care   ❐ refreshments

8. We agree to the following rules for our group:

   ❐ PRIORITY: While we are in this group, group meetings have priority.

   ❐ PARTICIPATION: Everyone is given the right to their own opinion and all questions are respected.

   ❐ CONFIDENTIALITY: Anything said in the meeting is not to be repeated outside the meeting.

   ❐ EMPTY CHAIR: The group stays open to new people and invites prospective members to visit the group.

   ❐ SUPPORT: Permission is given to call each other in times of need.

   ❐ ADVICE GIVING: Unsolicited advice is not allowed.

   ❐ MISSION: We will do all that is in our power to start a new group.

**Love the brotherhood.** While respect is to be shown to all, it is necessary to go beyond respect to love when it comes to one's fellow Christians.

**fear God.** The respect due God is, in fact, the "reverent fear" that Peter has already talked about in 1:17 (see note there).

**honor the king.** The kind of respect due the king is of a different sort. The word "fear" has religious connotations while "honor" is a secular term. This too was an amazing injunction. The king was the one responsible for the persecution they were experiencing!

**2:18 Slaves, submit yourselves.** Slaves were the legal property of their masters. This fact, though inherently wrong, nevertheless defined the reality within which they had to live. Peter (and other New Testament writers) does not counsel rebellion (it would have no chance of success at that point in history) or even "passive resistance" (which likewise would not work with masters who could, legally, take your life). What gave slaves the freedom to submit in this way is the sense that they as Christians were, in fact, members of a heavenly family and of a kingdom far more significant than the earthly reality within which they lived. Indeed, when the Lord returned (and they thought this would be quite soon), their true position would be revealed and they would live in this new reality for the age to come.

**with all respect.** This phrase is literally, "with all fear." This is not, however, fear toward the master (Peter rejects such a posture in 3:14) but reverence toward God who is their true Master (see also vv. 16–17).

**2:19 the pain of unjust suffering.** It was not easy to be a slave. Slaves were considered to be property and therefore their owners had absolute control over them. Although in the first century one did not find the kind of widespread brutality that prevailed in the 19th century slave trade, still slaves were the victims of much unjust treatment.

**2:21–25** Jesus is their model for the way to act in the face of injustice. Here, Peter is probably quoting from (or alluding to) an ancient creed, hymn or liturgy. This whole section echoes Isaiah 52:13–53:12.

**2:21 To this you were called, because Christ suffered for you.** The basis on which Peter says what he does about accepting unjust treatment is the example of Jesus who suffered for humankind. Christian slaves are to imitate Christ.

**2:22** Peter directly quotes Isaiah 53:9 to point out once again the sinlessness of Jesus (see 1:19). A slave would understand that innocence was no guarantee of just treatment.

**2:24** In a key passage about the atonement, Peter points out that Jesus was their representative. He bore their sins. He took upon himself the penalty which they deserved because of their sin.

**tree.** This is literally "wood" and was used both in the Old Testament (Deut. 21:23) and New Testament (Acts 5:30; Gal. 3:13) to refer to a means of punishment.

**so that.** Peter points to two results of Jesus' death on the cross: (1) because of it they are able to die to sin and (2) they can now live for righteousness. In other words, it is the moral impact of the Cross which Peter chooses to highlight here (and not the forgiveness of sin or remission of guilt which are also the result of the atonement). The death of Jesus makes it possible for them to leave their old lives of sin and follow instead a new way of life.

**wounds.** The Greek word refers to the welts and swelling which result from blows to the body with a fist or a whip.

**healed.** Christ's wounds brought restoration to their sin-scarred lives.

**2:25 returned.** They were once like lost sheep, but now they have been converted (i.e., they have turned around and come back to Christ).

**Shepherd.** This was a common Old Testament image: God was like a Shepherd calling together his wandering sheep. In the New Testament this title was applied to Jesus.

# 6 Wives & Husbands—1 Peter 3:1–7

## THREE-PART AGENDA

**ICE-BREAKER**
15 Minutes

**BIBLE STUDY**
30 Minutes

**CARING TIME**
15–45 Minutes

> **LEADER:** Check page M7 in the center section for a good ice-breaker, particularly if you have a new person at this meeting. Is your group working well together—with everyone "fielding their position" as shown on the team roster on page M5?

## TO BEGIN THE BIBLE STUDY TIME
(Choose 1 or 2)

1. How did you wear your hair when you were in high school?

2. What is your favorite piece of jewelry to wear?

3. If married, what is something you appreciate about your spouse?

## READ SCRIPTURE & DISCUSS
(If you don't have time for all the questions in this section, conclude the Bible Study [30 min.] by answering question #8.)

1. Who is the happiest married couple you know? What is the secret of their success?

2. *Women*: How do you feel about the standard set for wives in verse 1?

3. *Men*: How do you feel about the standard set for husbands in verse 7?

4. In practical terms, what does it mean for a wife to submit to her husband?

Wives and Husbands

**3** *Wives, in the same way be submissive to your husbands so that, if any of them do not believe the word, they may be won over without words by the behavior of their wives, ²when they see the purity and reverence of your lives. ³Your beauty should not come from outward adornment, such as braided hair and the wearing of gold jewelry and fine clothes. ⁴Instead, it should be that of your inner self, the unfading beauty of a gentle and quiet spirit, which is of great worth in God's sight. ⁵For this is the way the holy women of the past who put their hope in God used to make themselves beautiful. They were submissive to their own husbands, ⁶like Sarah, who obeyed Abraham and called him her master. You are her daughters if you do what is right and do not give way to fear.*

*⁷Husbands, in the same way be considerate as you live with your wives, and treat them with respect as the weaker partner and as heirs with you of the gracious gift of life, so that nothing will hinder your prayers.*

5. What powerful impact can a submissive spirit have on an unbelieving spouse?

6. In practical terms, in what ways can a husband be considerate to his wife and treat her with respect?

7. In our society, how does beauty tend to be defined? What qualities from this passage define beauty? How do these definitions compare?

8. What is the lesson in this passage for you?

## CARING TIME

(Choose 1 or 2 of these questions before closing in prayer. Be sure to pray for the empty chair.)

1. How is the group doing with its "team assignments" (review the team roster on p. M5)?

2. Congratulations! You are over halfway through this study. What do you look forward to when you come to this group?

3. How would you like the group to pray for you this week?

**Summary.** Peter continues his discussion of relationships. Peter's general principle is "respect for all," and thus far he has shown how this applies to the relationship between Christians and secular rulers and between Christian slaves and their masters. In this passage he looks at how wives and husbands are to relate to each other. Here Paul tells wives to respect their husbands (vv. 1–6) and husbands to respect their wives (v. 7). His particular concern is with Christian wives who have pagan husbands (vv. 1–4). What he says is based on principles drawn from the Old Testament (vv. 5–6). Peter's advice to wives is six times as long as that to husbands because in the first century when it came to marriage women faced, by far, a more difficult situation than men.

**3:1 *Wives.*** The position of wives in first-century society was not dissimilar to that of slaves. Under Jewish law a woman was a thing—she was owned by her husband in exactly the same way as he owned his sheep and his goats. Under no circumstances could she leave him, although he could dismiss her at any moment. Likewise, a woman had no rights under Roman law. When she was under her father she was under the *patria potestas,* the father's power, which gave the father even the right of life or death over her; and when she married she passed equally into the power of her husband. She was completely subject to her husband, and completely at his mercy (Barclay).

***in the same way.*** By this phrase Peter makes a transition from slaves to wives. Just as the behavior of Christ was the model for slaves, so too is it for women.

***be submissive.*** Again, as he did for slaves, Peter counsels submission, not rebellion. Between Christian husbands and wives this was "mutual submission" as Paul made clear (Eph. 5:21–33) and by definition mutual submission rules out hierarchal differences between spouses. But here Peter is thinking about marriage to a pagan husband who would consider himself in charge of his wife.

***if any of them do not believe.*** For a woman to become a Christian and so leave the faith of her husband was a revolutionary step in the first century which had the potential to produce grave problems.

***won over.*** Peter (like Paul) does not counsel Christian women to leave pagan husbands. His desire is that the husbands be converted. So he describes the kind of attitude and behavior on the part of the wife that has the potential to lead an unbelieving husband to faith.

**3:2 *purity and reverence.*** What the pagan husband will notice about his wife is how she lives now that she has become a Christian. In particular, he will note her "purity." This word refers not just to sexual purity (chaste behavior), but also to purity of thought, motive and action. He will see her "reverence" (i.e., that she has an awareness of God that causes her to live a good life).

**3:3 *outward adornment.*** Whether women should spend so much time and energy on clothes and jewelry was a question of some debate in the first century. In response, one Roman writer said that since women were allowed to do nothing else in society, they should be allowed this luxury. What Peter says here finds its root in the Old Testament (see Isa. 3:18–24 which lists various forms of adornment and comments that all this will pass away on the Day of Judgment).

> *Between Christian husbands and wives this was "mutual submission" as Paul made clear (Eph. 5:21–33) and by definition mutual submission rules out hierarchal differences between spouses. But here Peter is thinking about marriage to a pagan husband who would consider himself in charge of his wife.*

**3:4 *inner self.*** The true center of the personality; the unseen, secret personality; that which makes her who she really is.

**3:5 *holy women.*** They were "holy" not in the sense of being pious, but because they were chosen by God for his purposes.

**3:6 *like Sarah.*** The use of Sarah as an example of obedience shows that Peter was not devoid of a sense of humor. In Genesis, Abraham is shown as obeying Sarah as often as Sarah obeyed Abraham (see Gen. 16:2,6; 21:11–12). The point of Peter's reference to Sarah is that wives in the new covenant can learn from their spiritual ancestress. If Sarah submitted in obedience, the least her spiritual daughters can do is to submit in servanthood. Sarah obeyed Abraham, but Christian wives, her spiritual daughters, are never told to "obey" their husbands either here or anywhere else in the Bible. Instead, they are asked to "do what is right." Sarah called Abraham "lord," but Christian wives are never told to call their husbands "lord" anywhere in the Bible. Instead, they are told in this verse to "not give way to fear." "There is no fear in love. But perfect love drives out fear … " (1 John 4:18) (Bilezikian).

**3:7** In contrast to verses 1–2, where the focus is on Christian wives and pagan husbands, here Peter discusses how Christian husbands should relate to Christian wives. In the first century it was customary for the wife to adopt the religion of her husband, so that if he were converted to Christianity it is likely that she would be too. Peter seems to assume here that this would be the case. Peter reminds husbands that the respect they are to show to all people (2:17) is also due to their own wives. That a husband had any obligation to his wife was a startlingly new principle in the first century. For example, the Roman writer Cato said: "If you were to catch your wife in an act of infidelity, you can kill her with impunity without a trial; but, if she were to catch you, she would not venture to touch you with her finger, and, indeed, she has no right." This, however, was not the Christian ethic. Both Peter and Paul make a point of identifying the obligations of a husband to a wife (see Eph. 5:25–33).

***in the same way.*** As he did when he addressed wives (v. 1), here too, in addressing husbands, Peter harkens back to the example of Christ who voluntarily gave himself for the sake of others (2:21). "The servant attitude modeled by Christ and required of slaves and wives is also the example for husbands" (Bilezikian).

***be considerate.*** That a husband should think about how he treated his wife (and not simply demand his "rights") was a new notion in a society where a wife was considered to be property. The phrase means literally "live with them according to knowledge." By "knowledge" is meant "Christian insight and tact, a conscience sensitive to God's will" (Kelly).

***treat them with respect.*** This phrase is literally "assigning honor," and as such is a paradoxical statement (in that inferiors give "honor" to superiors—in this Roman setting, women were unquestionably the inferior party).

> ***"There is no fear in love. But perfect love drives out fear … ."***

***the weaker partner.*** Literally, the "weaker vessel." There has been much debate as to what this means. It might refer to anatomical differences between men and women (this phrase was used in Greek to refer to the woman's body), to the inferior position of women in that society, or to the comparative lack of physical strength on the part of the woman. By Peter's own example, it cannot mean inferiority spiritually or morally. His wife accompanied him on his preaching tours (1 Cor. 9:5) and according to a reliable tradition she joined him in death as a martyr.

***heirs with you.*** Literally, joint heirs or coheirs. Both husband and wife are equal participants in the grace of God, again reinforcing the idea of the new mutuality that has come to men and women who are in Christ.

***so that nothing will hinder your prayers.*** "Should husbands default in any of those areas by reverting to carnal, self-assertive ways, they might as well cease praying" (Bilezikian).

# 7 Suffering for Good—1 Peter 3:8–22

## THREE-PART AGENDA

| ICE-BREAKER | BIBLE STUDY | CARING TIME |
|---|---|---|
| 15 Minutes | 30 Minutes | 15–45 Minutes |

---

 **LEADER:** *To help you identify an Apprentice / Leader for a new small group (or if you have a new person at this meeting), see the listing of ice-breakers on page M7 of the center section.*

## TO BEGIN THE BIBLE STUDY TIME
(Choose 1 or 2)

1. What is something you are afraid of: Spiders? Snakes? Flying? The dark? Other?

2. As a child, what can you remember fighting about on family trips?

3. Who is usually the peacemaker in your family?

## READ SCRIPTURE & DISCUSS
(If you don't have time for all the questions in this section, conclude the Bible Study [30 min.] by answering question #7.)

1. What's a really good day you've had lately?

2. What instructions are given to "whoever would love life and see good days" (v. 10)?

3. In what way are you blessed "even if you should suffer for what is right" (v. 14)?

4. What is "the reason for the hope that you have" (v. 15)?

5. From this passage, why can a Christian be confident even in the midst of suffering?

### Suffering for Doing Good

*8Finally, all of you, live in harmony with one another; be sympathetic, love as brothers, be compassionate and humble. 9Do not repay evil with evil or insult with insult, but with blessing, because to this you were called so that you may inherit a blessing. 10For,*

> *"Whoever would love life*
>     *and see good days*
> *must keep his tongue from evil*
>     *and his lips from deceitful speech.*
> *11He must turn from evil and do good;*
>     *he must seek peace and pursue it.*
> *12For the eyes of the Lord are on the righteous*
>     *and his ears are attentive to their prayer,*
> *but the face of the Lord is against those who do evil."*a

*13Who is going to harm you if you are eager to do good? 14But even if you should suffer for what is right, you are blessed. "Do not fear what they fear; do not be frightened." 15But in your hearts set apart Christ as Lord. Always be prepared to give an answer to everyone who asks you to give the reason for the hope that you have. But do this with gentleness and respect, 16keeping a clear conscience, so that those who speak maliciously against your good behavior in Christ may be ashamed of their slander. 17It is better, if it is God's will, to suffer for doing good than for doing evil. 18For Christ died for sins once for all, the righteous for the unrighteous, to bring you to God. He was put to death in the body but made alive by the Spirit, 19through whom also he went and preached to the spirits in prison 20who disobeyed long ago when God waited patiently in the days of Noah while the ark was being built. In it only a few people, eight in all, were saved through water, 21and this water symbolizes baptism that now saves you also—not the removal of dirt from the body but the pledge of a good conscience toward God. It saves you by the resurrection of Jesus Christ, 22who has gone into heaven and is at God's right hand—with angels, authorities and powers in submission to him.*

a12 Psalm 34:12–16

6. When was the last time you had an opportunity to talk about your faith with a nonbeliever? How did you feel about it?

7. What relationship in your life needs more harmony right now? How can you bring harmony to this relationship?

## CARING TIME

(Choose 1 or 2 of these questions before closing in prayer.)

1. If this group is helping hold you accountable for something, how are you doing in that area? If not, what is something for which you would like this group to hold you accountable?

2. Have you started to work on your group mission— to choose an Apprentice / Leader from this group to start a new group in the future? (See Mission / Multiplication on p. M3.)

3. How can the group pray for you in the coming week?

# Notes—1 Peter 3:8–22

**Summary.** In the first paragraph of this passage (vv. 8–12) Peter concludes his comments on the nature of a missionary lifestyle. The question he has been dealing with is how they can "live such good lives among the pagans that, though they accuse you of doing wrong, they may see your good deeds and glorify God on the day he visits us" (2:12). His answer is that respect is the key to this kind of lifestyle. Respect is due the state through its duly appointed rulers (2:13–17), it is due slave owners even though they may not be kind to you as a slave (2:18–20); a wife is to respect her pagan husband even though he may consider her to be his property (3:1–6). Here in verses 8–12, by way of conclusion, he reiterates what he said in 2:17: respect both fellow believers (v. 8) and those who are your enemies (v. 9). In the second paragraph of this passage (vv. 13–22), Peter moves from urging respect for those who do evil to the evil itself which is being done to the Christians in Asia. He talks about suffering for doing good (vv. 13–17) and about how Christ is "an example not so much of a proper attitude toward suffering (though cf. 4:1!) as of the certainty of God's vindication. His victory over the 'disobedient spirits' makes possible the victory of Christians over their oppressors" (Michaels).

> *Christ died—as have men and women down through the ages. But his death was different in that it was a full, sufficient, and adequate sacrifice that atones for the sins of all people.*

**3:8–12** Peter ends his comments (begun back in 2:13) with some general advice concerning how they are to relate to one another and to the pagan community.

**3:8** By means of five exhortations Peter defines how they as Christians ought to treat each other.

**live in harmony.** The phrase is literally "all of one mind." By it Peter encourages the kind of unity that is vital in a hostile environment. There must be no divisions within the church.

**be sympathetic.** They must also be able to "enter into and share the feelings of others" (Kelly).

**love as brothers.** Peter uses the verb related to *philadelphia* (love amongst kin) instead of the more common verb related to *agape* (self-giving love). By it he encourages them to hold on to the kind of love that has knit them together as the family of Christ.

**be compassionate.** The Greek word used here is derived from the word for heart, kidney and liver, i.e., the internal organs. The Greeks thought these were the source of feelings. Peter is urging them to enter into the sufferings of others in their community with deep human emotion.

**humble.** This was not a virtue much prized by the Greeks. Humility was for slaves and as such was despised. However, the humility of Jesus (who had all power and voluntarily gave it up) became the model for Christians, so in the church humility came to be seen in a positive light.

**3:9** Peter tells them not to retaliate against those who persecute them.

**blessing.** Instead, they are to bless their persecutors! This reinforces the advice he has given in the rest of this section. They are to act in unexpected ways.

**3:10–12** Once again Peter refers back to Psalm 34 (see 2:3), where the theme is that the Lord will rescue his suffering children who trust in him.

**3:13–17** Having pointed out how they are to relate to those who oppress them, now Peter looks directly at the oppression itself and how they are to respond to it. He reassures them that, in the end, righteous behavior will be vindicated. Even if they are persecuted, they are not to fear. Instead, they must focus inwardly on Jesus while outwardly displaying good behavior.

**3:14 But.** Peter does not mislead them, however. There is no assurance that good behavior will invariably shield them from harm.

**blessed.** If they do suffer, rather than being downcast, they are to count this as a privilege.

**Do not fear ...** Quoting Isaiah 8:12, Peter points out that the real danger is fear. "Do not fear what they fear" could also be translated, "Do not fear their threats."

**3:15 But.** Instead of fear in their hearts, they need to place Jesus there.

**in your hearts.** At the core of their being Christ must reign.

**set apart Christ.** Literally, "sanctify" Christ. Christ is to be acknowledged as holy and worshiped as Lord. They are to open themselves to his inner presence.

**be prepared to give an answer.** Although this may refer to an official inquiry in which they are called upon to defend the fact that they are Christians, it probably is more general in reference. When anybody asks about the hope they have, they are to explain why they are followers of Jesus.

**the reason.** Greeks valued a logical, intelligent statement as to why one held certain beliefs.

**with gentleness and respect.** This reply should not be given in a contentious or defensive way. Their response should be "without arrogance or self-assertion, with due respect and deference towards men, and with proper awe and reverence before God" (Stibbs).

**3:16 a clear conscience.** The inner awareness of what is right morally. If they are living in the way Peter describes, they will have nothing to hide; there will be no guilt to make them defensive.

**3:18–22** The reason why they can be so confident in the face of suffering is because of the victory Christ has won over death. Furthermore, if they do suffer, they are simply walking the same path as their Lord.

**3:18 died for sins.** Christ died—as have men and women down through the ages. But his death was different in that it was a full, sufficient, and adequate sacrifice that atones for the sins of all people.

**once for all.** The sacrifices in the temple had to be repeated over and over again; Christ's sacrifice was the final and perfect sacrifice through which all people in all ages find salvation.

**the righteous for the unrighteous.** His death was vicarious; i.e., he died in the place of others.

**bring you to God.** It is because of Christ's death that they are restored to a right relationship with God.

**3:19 preached.** The nature of Jesus' proclamation has been interpreted as: (1) the Gospel which is proclaimed to those who lived before Christ came, or as (2) the announcement to the rebellious spirits that their power has been broken.

**the spirits.** Who these spirits are is not clear. They have been variously identified as: (1) sinners who lived before the incarnation of Christ, or (2) the rebellious angels of Genesis 6:1–4.

> *Even if they are persecuted, they are not to fear. Instead, they must focus inwardly on Jesus while outwardly displaying good behavior.*

**prison.** Likewise, the nature of this prison is not clear. It has been identified as: (1) hell, (2) a metaphor for the imprisonment that sin and ignorance brings, or (3) the world of spirits.

**3:20–21** His next reference is to the Flood. Again, it is not clear what exactly Peter is saying.

**3:20 eight in all.** Noah and his wife and their three sons (Shem, Ham and Japheth) along with their wives.

**3:21 symbolizes.** Peter is using metaphors to explain spiritual truth.

**the pledge of a good conscience.** In baptism, they accepted the privileges and responsibilities of following Christ. "Pledge" could also be translated "response."

**saves you by the resurrection.** It is not the baptism in and of itself through which they found salvation. It is via Jesus they are saved. It is to the resurrected Jesus they pledge themselves. It is the resurrection life of Jesus which they experience.

# 8 Living for God—1 Peter 4:1–11

## THREE-PART AGENDA

| **ICE-BREAKER** | **BIBLE STUDY** | **CARING TIME** |
| 15 Minutes | 30 Minutes | 15–45 Minutes |

>  **LEADER: To help you identify people who might form the core of a new small group (or if a new person comes to this meeting), see the listing of ice-breakers on page M7 of the center section.**

## TO BEGIN THE BIBLE STUDY TIME
(Choose 1 or 2)

1. If you could add one hour to your day, how would you put it to use?

2. What is something that seems to be "all the rage" but which you don't have an interest in?

3. When is a time you have been in great physical pain?

## READ SCRIPTURE & DISCUSS
(If you don't have time for all the questions in this section, conclude the Bible Study [30 min.] by answering question #7.)

1. In what ways have your priorities changed as you have gotten older?

2. How can suffering change a person's life for the better? How have you seen this to be true in your own life?

3. Why would the radical change in lifestyle of the Christians be so upsetting to their pagan friends or family? When has someone heaped "abuse on you" (v. 4) because of something you wouldn't join them in doing?

## Living for God

**4** Therefore, since Christ suffered in his body, arm your-selves also with the same attitude, because he who has suffered in his body is done with sin. *²As a result, he does not live the rest of his earthly life for evil human desires, but rather for the will of God. ³For you have spent enough time in the past doing what pagans choose to do—living in debauchery, lust, drunkenness, orgies, carousing and detestable idolatry. ⁴They think it strange that you do not plunge with them into the same flood of dissipation, and they heap abuse on you. ⁵But they will have to give account to him who is ready to judge the living and the dead. ⁶For this is the reason the gospel was preached even to those who are now dead, so that they might be judged according to men in regard to the body, but live according to God in regard to the spirit.*

*⁷The end of all things is near. Therefore be clear minded and self-controlled so that you can pray. ⁸Above all, love each other deeply, because love covers over a multitude of sins. ⁹Offer hospitality to one another without grumbling. ¹⁰Each one should use whatever gift he has received to serve others, faithfully administering God's grace in its var-ious forms. ¹¹If anyone speaks, he should do it as one speaking the very words of God. If anyone serves, he should do it with the strength God provides, so that in all things God may be praised through Jesus Christ. To him be the glory and the power for ever and ever. Amen.*

4. How does your lifestyle differ from that of your non-Christian friends? From verses 7–10, what are some priorities that a Christian should have in their life?

5. If you were to rate your-self on the "love meter" from 1 (shallow) to 10 (deep), how have you been doing at showing love to others lately?

6. What standard does Peter set for us in this passage regarding what we say and do?

7. What is something you or this group can plan on doing in service to some-one else?

## CARING TIME

(Choose 1 or 2 of these questions before closing in prayer.)

1. How are you doing at spending personal time in prayer and Bible study?

2. Who would you choose as the leader if this group "gave birth" to a new small group? Who else would you choose to be a part of the leadership core for a new group?

3. In what specific way can the group pray for you this week?

**Summary.** The vindication that will be theirs is coming, Peter says in this passage. Their sinful past is behind them. They do not have to face judgment on that account. And through Christ they will prevail over their tormentors (vv. 1–6). Furthermore, the end is near (v. 7). This being the case, they must strive to live out a lifestyle that is consistent with their calling (vv. 7–9), faithfully using the gifts of grace given them by God (vv. 10–11).

**4:1–6** This is a difficult passage to interpret. However, it is clear that Peter is reassuring these Asian Christians that despite the suffering they face they will prevail because of their identification in baptism with Jesus' death and resurrection.

**4:1 *in his body.*** A single Greek word which means literally, "in the flesh." It is repeated four times in verses 1–6. When it is first used ("Christ suffered in his body"), Peter probably has in mind the death of Christ. This also seems to be true when he says, "he who has suffered in his body is done with sin." Death is the only form of suffering that ends sinning permanently. In the case of Christ who was without sin, his death ended his identification with the sins of the world. Through his death he won a victory over sin on behalf of humanity (Stibbs).

**4:2** The "attitude" with which Christians are to "arm" themselves (v. 1) is stated here. That which determines the lifestyle of one who has been baptized into the death of Jesus is the will of God, not the desires of the flesh.

**4:3** The list of vices here parallels the lists in Romans 13:13 and Galatians 5:19–21. The picture it paints is of a lifestyle characterized by sexual and alcoholic excess based on idolatry. This is a lifestyle out of control, arranged around harmful addictions and cultic practices.

***time in the past.*** Christians have two views of time: time past, in which they gave themselves over to a destructive lifestyle, and "the rest of ... earthly life" (v. 2), that time following conversion in which they live in accord with God's will.

***doing what pagans choose to do.*** The Christians to whom Peter writes are Gentiles rather than Jews, as this phrase shows.

***debauchery.*** "Excesses;" "outrages against decency;" "living in sensualities."

***drunkenness.*** Literally, "overflowings of wine."

***carousing.*** Literally, "drinking bouts;" "drunken parties."

**4:4** Their pagan friends are astonished that they no longer lead this out-of-control lifestyle, but then their amazement turns into reaction and abuse.

***abuse.*** There is plenty of evidence, from pagan as well as Christian sources, that it was precisely the reluctance of Christians to participate in the routine of contemporary life, particularly conventionally accepted amusements, civic ceremonies, and any function involving contact with idolatry or what they considered immorality, that caused them to be hated, despised and themselves suspected of illicit practices (Kelly).

> The final judgment will include both those who are still alive when Christ returns and those who have already died. All will face judgment.

**4:5** This attitude will bring its own reward. These abusive pagans will themselves face judgment for their actions.

***they will have to give account to him.*** "Those who do not receive Him as their Saviour, must face Him as their Judge" (Stibbs).

***the living and the dead.*** The final judgment will include both those who are still alive when Christ returns and those who have already died. All will face judgment.

**4:6 *the gospel was preached even to those who are now dead.*** The meaning of this phrase has been much debated. It probably refers to those members of the church who heard and accepted the Gospel but who have since died. Some scholars, however, connect this verse to 3:19–20 and conclude this is a reference to Christ's descent into hell, during which he proclaimed the Gospel to those who were there. Some assert that those who heard

Christ were those who lived prior to his coming and so never had a chance to hear the Gospel. Others feel that all the dead get the chance to hear the Gospel (and hence receive a second chance to come to faith). However, there is no necessary connection between 3:19–20 and this verse; and in any case, the reference in 3:19 is to "spirits" while the reference here is to human beings who have died.

*judged according to men in regard to the body.* This phrase may mean that death itself is a form of judgment. The body dies because it is sinful. This is "the last, remaining sting of sin which they have to suffer," i.e., "the death of their sinful and mortal earthly bodies. Beyond that lies spiritual quickening, and entrance into fuller life." For those who become Christians, "the judgment due to them as sinners is fully accomplished in this world, i.e., *in the flesh*; and *in the spirit*, both here and still more beyond death, they enter into life, and find themselves, through Christ's physical death and spiritual quickening, truly brought into God's presence" (Stibbs).

**4:7–11** Peter gives yet another reason for forsaking their old, self-indulgent lifestyle: history is about to end. This is the time, he says, for self-discipline, prayer, and active love. In particular, they must care for each other. Mutuality is the key: mutual love (v. 8), mutual hospitality (v. 9), and mutual ministry (vv. 10–11).

**4:7** *The end of all things.* The second coming of Jesus will mark the close of history when this world as it is now known passes away.

*be clear minded and self-controlled.* As history draws to a close, their temptation might be to let their excitement get out of hand or to become self-indulgent.

*so that you can pray.* When people are not thinking clearly or when their lives are out of control, they cannot pray properly.

---

*The second coming of Jesus will mark the close of history when this world as it is now known passes away.*

---

**4:8** Love is the key to a last-days' lifestyle.

*love covers over a multitude of sins.* A paraphrase of Proverbs 10:12. People tend to forgive those whom they love.

**4:9** *Offer hospitality.* This is one concrete way to show love. In a day when there were few decent hotels (most hotels were expensive, dirty and bawdy), travelers depended on the willingness of others to take them in.

**4:10** *gift.* This word is *charisma* and refers to the different gifts which the Holy Spirit gives to individual Christians for the sake of the whole body.

*to serve others.* The point of these gifts is to use them for the sake of others.

*God's grace in its various forms.* "Each one" has a gift, but not all have the same gift. (See Rom. 12:6–8; 1 Cor. 12:7–10; Eph. 4:11–12 for lists of various gifts.)

**4:11** Peter discusses two gifts in particular: the gift of teaching and preaching and the gift of service.

*If anyone speaks.* This is not the gift of tongues (ecstatic utterance, glossolalia) nor the gift of prophecy. The Greek word here refers to preaching and teaching.

*as one speaking the very words of God.* Barclay paraphrases this: "If a man has the duty of preaching, let him preach not as a man offering his own opinions or propagating his own prejudices, but as a man with a message from God."

*If anyone serves.* There are different kinds of service: helping those in need, giving leadership, providing money (see Acts 6:1–4; Rom. 12:13; 1 Cor. 12:5).

*so that in all things God may be praised.* The purpose of these gifts is to glorify God through their exercise, not to bring glory to the one with the gift.

# 9 Suffering for Christ—1 Peter 4:12–19

## THREE-PART AGENDA

**ICE-BREAKER**
15 Minutes

**BIBLE STUDY**
30 Minutes

**CARING TIME**
15–45 Minutes

> *LEADER: Has your group discussed its plans on what to study after this course is finished? What about the mission project described on page M6 in the center section?*

## TO BEGIN THE BIBLE STUDY TIME
(Choose 1 or 2)

1. As a kid, when it came to getting a shot at the doctor's office, how brave were you?

2. When it comes to dealing with pain, who's the biggest wimp in your family?

3. Who is someone that has been an encourager to you through a difficult time?

## READ SCRIPTURE & DISCUSS
(If you don't have time for all the questions in this section, conclude the Bible Study [30 min.] by answering question #7.)

1. When have you been in a situation where being a Christian wasn't very popular or accepted?

2. What false assumption does Peter set straight in verse 12? How often are you surprised at the trials of life?

3. From this passage, what attitude should a Christian have toward suffering?

4. How is *rejoicing* in suffering different from just *enduring* suffering? Does God really expect you to be *glad* you suffer? What is meant by "rejoice"?

## Suffering for Being a Christian

*[12]Dear friends, do not be surprised at the painful trial you are suffering, as though something strange were happening to you. [13]But rejoice that you participate in the sufferings of Christ, so that you may be overjoyed when his glory is revealed. [14]If you are insulted because of the name of Christ, you are blessed, for the Spirit of glory and of God rests on you. [15]If you suffer, it should not be as a murderer or thief or any other kind of criminal, or even as a meddler. [16]However, if you suffer as a Christian, do not be ashamed, but praise God that you bear that name. [17]For it is time for judgment to begin with the family of God; and if it begins with us, what will the outcome be for those who do not obey the gospel of God? [18]And,*

> *"If it is hard for the righteous to be saved,*
>     *what will become of the ungodly and the sinner?"*[a]

*[19]So then, those who suffer according to God's will should commit themselves to their faithful Creator and continue to do good.*

[a]18 Prov. 11:31

5. In verse 19, how does Peter summarize what Christians should do during times of suffering? When you are going through an intense struggle, do you find it easy—or difficult—to "commit" yourself to your "faithful Creator"?

6. What effect has past suffering had on your commitment to God?

7. How can you be an encourager to someone this week who is going through a difficult time?

## CARING TIME

(Answer all the questions that follow, then close in prayer.)

1. Next week will be your last session in this study. How would you like to celebrate: A dinner? A party? Other?

2. What is the next step for this group: Start a new group? Continue with another study?

3. What prayer needs or praises would you like to share?

(If the group plans to continue, see the back inside cover of this book for what is available from Serendipity.)

**Summary.** Peter now moves into the final section of his letter in which he addresses the challenge facing these Asian Christians. He begins in this passage by focusing on the "painful trial" (or "fiery ordeals" as the New English Bible puts it) they are going through. He does not introduce any new themes. Rather, he summarizes what he has already said in an intense and direct way as he encourages them to carry on in the face of their suffering. Suffering ought not to surprise them (v. 12), Peter says, nor should they be ashamed if they do suffer (v. 16). (He assumes that such suffering is because they bear the name of Christ, not because of wrongdoing.) Instead, they must rejoice (v. 13) and praise God (v. 16), knowing that they are participating in the sufferings of Christ (v. 13) and that the glory of God rests on them (v. 14). Furthermore, what they are going through is a sign that the end times have begun (v. 17). (They know that these will culminate in the return of Christ at which point their suffering will end.) They must remember that even though they are going through a hard time (v. 17) a far worse judgment will come upon their persecutors (vv. 17–18).

**4:12–14** Both suffering and glory mark the life of the Christian. The glory is both in the future (v. 13) and in the present (v. 14).

**4:12 *Dear friends.*** With this form of address Peter begins the final section of his letter. The note of encouragement that he will sound in these remaining verses begins with this phrase. By it he reminds them once again that they are part of a loving fellowship.

***do not be surprised.*** In 4:4 he comments that their persecutors "think it strange" that they do not participate any longer in a debauched lifestyle. Here he uses the same verb but now it is their turn to be astonished. What they should not be surprised about is that they are persecuted. "It was a poignant problem to Christians in the apostolic age, especially those who had emerged from a Gentile background, that they should be misunderstood, disliked and subjected to insults and ill-treatment, when they knew themselves to be striving to carry out God's will" (Kelly).

***painful trial.*** This word means "burning." It was used to describe cooking something over a fire or purifying a metal by fire. It is a vivid way to describe

what was happening to them. This is the fourth time Peter has mentioned their trials (see also 1:6–7; 2:19–23; 3:13–17).

**4:13 *rejoice.*** Rather than being bewildered ("surprised") at what is happening to them, they are actively to rejoice. They are not merely to passively endure these trials. They must come to understand them as a way to participate in the experience of their Lord. This verb is in the present tense, signifying that what Peter is calling for is not a single such response but an ongoing, continuous attitude of joy. This same attitude toward suffering is also found in Paul's epistle to the Philippians where joy is the central theme.

***participate.*** In 2:20–21 Peter said that they were called to follow in Christ's steps. This they do when they suffer, even though they have only done what is good. In 4:1 he went a step further by reminding them that in their baptism they share in the death of Christ. Here he ties all this together by declaring that in this way they participate in the sufferings of Christ.

***sufferings / glory.*** The connection between suffering and glory is made at other points in the New Testament (see Luke 6:22–23; Rom. 8:17; 2 Cor. 1:5–7; Phil. 3:10–11).

***when his glory is revealed.*** Peter has already reminded them that "the end of all things is near" (4:7). An awareness of this reality will enable them to cope with their suffering, not only because they know that their persecutors will one day have to answer to God for their deeds (4:5,17–18) but because at that point in time they will come into their share of the glory of Christ (see also 1:13). Once again, Peter looks forward to the day when Jesus returns and believers experience salvation fully.

**4:14 *If you are insulted because of the name of Christ, you are blessed.*** The glory they experience is not only in the future. It is also in the here and now.

***the Spirit of glory and of God rests on you.*** Through the Holy Spirit they experience the glory of God (see 1:6,8).

***glory.*** In the Old Testament, the primary meaning of this word (*kabod*) is that of weight and substance. A man of wealth is a man of substance, of *kabod*. His external appearance and bearing would, in nine cases out of 10, reflect his wealth, and also be called *kabod*. His wealth and dignity demanded and compelled respect and honor from his fellows, and this was called glory or honor. Hence weight, substance, wealth, dignity, noble bearing, and honor all contributed to its meaning. To these fundamental meanings Ezekiel added that of brightness (Alan Richardson). This word came to describe the actual, visible radiance of God himself. Glory is not just what God reflects; it is who he is. So in other words, these Asian Christians will (and do) share in the very nature of God himself.

**4:15** Not all suffering brings glory. Those that suffer because of wrongdoing do not gain this blessing. Peter's point (which he already made in 2:20) is that it is one thing to be punished for committing a crime (which was not why these Asian Christians were being persecuted), and quite another to be punished for doing good (which is what was happening to them).

***murderer / thief / criminal.*** Each term connotes a recognizable form of wrongdoing which the civil authorities would clearly be justified in punishing (see 2:14).

***meddler.*** It is not clear to what this word refers. Some have translated it as "agitator" or "spy," implying revolutionary activity against Rome. But there is no evidence that this term even meant that. "We can only speculate what kind of meddling the writer has in mind (excessive zeal for making converts? causing discord in family or commercial life? over-eager denunciation of pagan habits? prying curiosity?), but [the author] plainly regards it as disreputable" (Kelly).

**4:16** ***Christian.*** Apart from two references in Acts (11:26 and 26:28), this is the only other use of "Christian" in the New Testament.

> *Not all suffering brings glory. Those that suffer because of wrongdoing do not gain this blessing. Peter's point is that it is one thing to be punished for committing a crime (which was not why these Asian Christians were being persecuted), and quite another to be punished for doing good (which is what was happening to them).*

**4:17** ***it is time for judgment to begin with the family of God.*** It was understood that in the last days the chosen people would suffer. This idea is found in the teaching of Jesus (Mark 13:8–13). In a sense, this is an encouraging sign. The tumultuous end times will precede the Second Coming, when it will be all over. When Christ returns, their inheritance and glory will begin.

***what will the outcome be for those who do not obey the gospel of God?*** The judgment will also reach out to those who disobey God. By implication, this judgment will be far worse (see also 2 Thess. 1:5–10).

**4:18** Peter confirms what he is saying by reference to Proverbs 11:31.

**4:19** ***commit themselves.*** This is a technical term which refers to the act of depositing money with a trusted friend. This is the same word Jesus used in Luke 23:46: "Father, into your hands I commit my spirit." In the end it all comes down to this. Those who suffer for doing good, those who suffer only because they are Christians (v. 16), must simply commit themselves to God. He is that trusted friend who can be relied upon absolutely to bear this trust. They will be safe with him.

# 10 Christian Attitude—1 Peter 5:1–14

## THREE-PART AGENDA

**ICE-BREAKER**
15 Minutes

**BIBLE STUDY**
30 Minutes

**CARING TIME**
15–45 Minutes

 *LEADER: Check page M7 of the center section for a good ice-breaker for this last session.*

## TO BEGIN THE BIBLE STUDY TIME
(Choose 1 or 2)

1. What do you do when you are anxious or stressed out: Bite your nails? Eat? Stop eating? Withdraw? Pray?

2. Growing up, who was your best friend? What made them so special?

3. What teacher or leader do you have a great deal of respect for and why?

## READ SCRIPTURE & DISCUSS
(If you don't have time for all the questions in this section, conclude the Bible Study [30 min.] by answering question #7.)

1. How has this group, or someone in the group, been a blessing to you over the course of this study?

2. Who is someone in your life who has "taken you under their wing" and helped you along the way?

3. What is Peter warning church leaders about? What guidelines does this passage provide for those in Christian leadership?

4. What anxiety in your life do you need to turn over to God? In what way does the promise in verse 10 give you encouragement?

## To Elders and Young Men

**5** *To the elders among you, I appeal as a fellow elder, a witness of Christ's sufferings and one who also will share in the glory to be revealed: ²Be shepherds of God's flock that is under your care, serving as overseers—not because you must, but because you are willing, as God wants you to be; not greedy for money, but eager to serve; ³not lording it over those entrusted to you, but being examples to the flock. ⁴And when the Chief Shepherd appears, you will receive the crown of glory that will never fade away.*

*⁵Young men, in the same way be submissive to those who are older. All of you, clothe yourselves with humility toward one another, because,*

> *"God opposes the proud*
> *but gives grace to the humble."*a

*⁶Humble yourselves, therefore, under God's mighty hand, that he may lift you up in due time. ⁷Cast all your anxiety on him because he cares for you.*

*⁸Be self-controlled and alert. Your enemy the devil prowls around like a roaring lion looking for someone to devour. ⁹Resist him, standing firm in the faith, because you know that your brothers throughout the world are undergoing the same kind of sufferings.*

*¹⁰And the God of all grace, who called you to his eternal glory in Christ, after you have suffered a little while, will himself restore you and make you strong, firm and steadfast. ¹¹To him be the power for ever and ever. Amen.*

## Final Greetings

*¹²With the help of Silas,ᵇ whom I regard as a faithful brother, I have written to you briefly, encouraging you and testifying that this is the true grace of God. Stand fast in it.*

*¹³She who is in Babylon, chosen together with you, sends you her greetings, and so does my son Mark. ¹⁴Greet one another with a kiss of love.*

*Peace to all of you who are in Christ.*

---

a5 Prov. 3:34          b12 Greek *Silvanus,* a variant of *Silas*

5. In this passage, who is identified as the enemy? What are we told about this enemy? How are we to guard against this enemy?

6. In this study of First Peter, what has been the key thing you have learned?

7. On a scale of 1 (baby steps) to 10 (giant leaps), how has your relationship with God progressed over the last three months?

## CARING TIME
(Answer all the questions that follow, then close in prayer.)

1. What will you remember most about this group?

2. What has the group decided to do next? What is the next step for you personally?

3. How would you like the group to continue to pray for you?

**Summary.** Peter ends his letter by addressing the question of how the church ought to function during a time of suffering (vv. 1–11). First, he examines the responsibilities of the elders (vv. 1–4). Second, he looks briefly at the responsibilities of younger church members (v. 5). Then, third, he comments on the responsibilities of all church members (vv. 6–7). Finally, he concludes by reminding them that they are, in fact, engaged in spiritual warfare (vv. 8–11). Satan is behind all their troubles. He ends his letter in typical fashion with personal greetings and a benediction (vv. 12–14).

> *The idea that the people of God are like a flock of sheep (and that their leaders are like shepherds) is found in a number of places in the Old Testament.*

**5:1–4** Peter has specific instructions for the leaders of the fellowship. It will not be easy for them to lead a church that is under fire.

**5:1 *elders.*** The leaders of the local congregation who probably functioned much in the same way as did the board of elders in a synagogue (i.e., they had administrative and spiritual responsibility for the congregation).

***a fellow elder.*** Peter bears the same sort of responsibility they do. Thus he understands the pressures and the problems they face.

***a witness.*** The Greek word is *martus,* from which "martyr" is derived. Strictly speaking, what Peter is saying is that he was an eyewitness of the death of Jesus. He is therefore able to point to Jesus in his suffering as an example they are to follow (2:21). In the New Testament, this word came to mean one who bears witness to Jesus (see Luke 24:48; Acts 1:8; 22:15). Eventually it was applied to those who suffered because of their witness (Acts 22:20; Rev. 2:13; 11:3,7). Thus it came into English as "martyr."

**5:2–3** Peter identifies those aspects of the elders' job that require special attention in troubled times. In this passage we get some insight into the role of elders in the first century.

**5:2 *Be shepherds.*** This is a command. They cannot be passive or slack in what they do. They need to attend to their job of caring for God's people.

***God's flock.*** The idea that the people of God are like a flock of sheep (and that their leaders are like shepherds) is found in a number of places in the Old Testament (see Ps. 23; Isa. 40:11; Jer. 23:1–4; Ezek. 34).

***serving as overseers.*** This was the main job of an elder: supervising the affairs of the community. This phrase later came to mean "function as a bishop." Peter follows this general admonition with three phrases, each expressed in an antithetical way, by which he defines the spirit in which they are to hold this office.

***not because you must, but because you are willing.*** The first of three antitheses. Here the contrast is between reluctant and willing service. The elders should be willing volunteers in God's service.

***not greedy for money, but eager to serve.*** The second antithesis: between service in order to profit financially and service based on zeal for God. In all likelihood, elders received some financial remuneration (see 1 Cor. 9:7–12; 1 Tim. 5:17–18). The temptation might be to regard their office simply as a job and not as a calling.

**5:3 *not lording it over those entrusted to you, but being examples.*** The third antithesis: between domineering those you are to care for or coming to them in humility. Peter has already defined how the community ought to function (see 2:13–3:12). Mutual respect, submission, humility and love are the attitudes which should characterize the Christian community, and the elders would be expected to set an example in displaying these attitudes.

***those entrusted to you.*** This phrase probably refers to splitting up the flock into groups, each of which would be under the care of a particular elder.

**5:4 *Chief Shepherd.*** Peter has already described Jesus as the "Shepherd" (2:25). Here he adds an adjective that reminds the elders that their authority is not absolute, but derived from Jesus.

**the crown of glory.** The victor at an athletic event in a Greek city had a garland of ivy or bay placed on his head. Citizens who performed outstanding service to the city were also given such crowns. The image of the crown became a common New Testament symbol for the reward promised to Christians (see 1 Cor. 9:25; 2 Tim. 4:8; James 1:12; Rev. 2:10). Peter says that this crown will consist of the "glory" of Christ which will be revealed at the Second Coming.

> *Mutual respect, submission, humility and love are the attitudes which should characterize the Christian community and the elders would be expected to set an example in displaying these attitudes.*

**5:5 Young men.** The Greek social order was such that young men were considered subordinate to older men.

**in the same way.** Probably a reference to 2:13–3:12, where Peter considered the question of how to relate to those who are above you in the social order. In that earlier section, the question was how to relate to those in secular society who have the potential to oppress you (rulers, slave owners, pagan husbands). Here the issue is how to relate to those in the church who are leaders.

**be submissive.** Submission and respect are called for once again.

**those who are older.** This is the same word that is translated "elders" in verse 1. In fact, the elders (leaders) would most likely have been chosen from those who were older in age.

**clothe yourselves with humility.** This is a rare verb, meaning "wrap yourselves" or "gird yourselves." It is derived from the name for the apron which was worn by slaves when working. It conjures up an image of Jesus who wrapped a towel around himself when he washed the feet of the disciples (John 13:4), an act which is the perfect demonstration of what humility is all about. There is an untranslated word which begins this sentence (*pantes* or "all") which marks a shift in focus from a brief admonition to younger men to instructions for all Christians.

**5:6 Humble yourselves.** The same humility which is owed one another is owed God as well.

**that he may lift you up in due time.** This will happen when Christ returns and they experience his glory.

**5:7 Cast all your anxiety on him.** This verb should be translated as a participle ("casting"), not as an imperative ("cast"), since in Greek it is connected to the imperative "humble yourself." It is not a separate commandment. "The true Christian attitude is not negative self-abandonment or resignation, but involves as the expression of one's self-humbling the positive entrusting of oneself and one's troubles to God" (Kelly).

**5:8 Be self-controlled and alert.** That they are not to be passive in the face of trouble is seen in this command. Coupled with conscious reliance on God, there must also be diligent effort on their part.

**the devil.** Behind all their trials stands the devil (*diabolos*). In the Old Testament he is known by the Hebrew name Satan. In the New Testament he is seen as the one who tempts (as he did with Jesus), as the Prince of Evil who rebelled against God, as the Antichrist, and as the one who seeks to undo God's purposes.

**5:9 Resist him.** Peter's advice is plain: do not run away, stand your ground and face him, refuse to give in to his purposes, trust in God (see also Eph. 6:10–13; James 4:7; Rev. 12:9–11).

**your brothers throughout the world are undergoing the same kind of sufferings.** Solidarity with Christian brothers and sisters around the world is a strong motivation for standing firm.

**5:10–11** Satan may be their enemy and he is powerful and vicious ("like a roaring lion looking for someone to devour"), but he is no match for God. Assurance of strength and victory is another motivation for continuing to resist evil.

**5:12–14** Peter concludes his letter—as do most letters in the New Testament—with greetings and personal comments.

**5:12** *Silas.* Like Paul (and others), Peter used an amanuensis (secretary/scribe) to write this letter. In this case, Silas seems to have had an active part in shaping the final form of the letter with its rather polished Greek. The Silas referred to here is probably Paul's companion on his second missionary trip (Acts 15:40–18:5), a minister of the Gospel (2 Cor. 1:19), and the coauthor with Paul of 1 and 2 Thessalonians.

*this is the true grace of God. Stand fast in it.* "The message of First Peter is that what the readers are experiencing is, in fact, the grace of God (cf. 1:13). In it they must stand" (Michaels).

**5:13** *She who is in Babylon ... sends you her greetings.* Peter is (probably) referring to the church (see 2 John 1,13) in Rome, where he was when he wrote this letter.

*my son Mark.* Tradition has it that Mark was another of Peter's secretaries; and, in writing the Gospel that bears his name, Mark was expressing Peter's experience of Jesus. Certainly this phrase reflects a warm relationship between the two.

> *"The true Christian attitude is not negative self-abandonment or resignation, but involves as the expression of one's self-humbling the positive entrusting of oneself and one's troubles to God."*

**5:14** *a kiss of love.* At some point during the worship service, Christians would greet each other with an embrace, signifying their close bonds as brothers and sisters in the Lord. This was a ritual developed by the church (and not, as in so many other cases, adopted from Jewish liturgy).

# Acknowledgments

It is not possible to write notes such as these without building upon the work of many scholars. In fact, our role has been primarily that of "translators"—standing between the commentaries and technical literature on the one hand and the needs of lay Christians on the other hand. Ample use has been made of the usual research tools in the field of New Testament studies, such as *A Greek-English Lexicon of the New Testament* (Bauer, Arndt & Gingrich), *Interpreter's Dictionary of the Bible, The New International Dictionary of New Testament Theology* (Colin Brown), *The Macmillan Bible Atlas* (Aharoni & Avi-Yonah), as well as other standard reference materials. In addition, use has been made of various commentaries. While it is not possible, given the scope and aim of this book, to acknowledge in detail the input of each author, the source of direct quotes and special insights is identified. The original author's name is noted in the parenthesis that follows the citation. Bibliographical data is listed below.

There were three commentaries in particular that were especially useful in writing these notes. These are *The Letters of James and Peter (The Daily Study Bible)*, William Barclay, Philadelphia: The Westminster Press, 1960; *A Commentary on the Epistles of Peter and Jude (Thornapple Commentaries)*, J. N. D. Kelly, Grand Rapids, MI: Baker Book House, 1981 (first published in 1969); and *The First Epistle General of Peter (Tyndale New Testament Commentaries)*, Alan M. Stibbs, London: The Tyndale Press, 1957.

The outline which was followed for 1 Peter is the work of J. Ramsey Michaels, formerly of Gordon Conwell Theological Seminary (taken from a handout used in his 1980 class on 1 Peter). In seeking to understand what Peter was saying about marriage roles, use was made of *Beyond Sex Roles*, by Gilbert Bilezikian, Grand Rapids, MI: Baker Book House, 1985.

Other commentaries that were referred to include: F.W. Beare, *The First Epistle of Peter* (3rd edition), Oxford, 1970; Ernest Best, *1 Peter (The New Century Bible Commentary)*, Grand Rapids, MI: Wm. Eerdmans Publishing Co.,1971; A.R.C. Leaney,*The Letters of Peter and Jude (The Cambridge Bible Commentary)*, Cambridge, England: Cambridge University Press, 1967; and Edward Gordon Selwyn, *The First Epistle of St. Peter (Thornapple Commentaries)*, Grand Rapids, MI: Baker Book House, 1981.

# Caring Time Notes

# Caring Time Notes

# Caring Time Notes